Anonymous

Summer Excursions for 1874 Via the Lehigh Valley Railroad

Anonymous

Summer Excursions for 1874 Via the Lehigh Valley Railroad

ISBN/EAN: 9783337419561

Printed in Europe, USA, Canada, Australia, Japan

Cover: Foto ©Andreas Hilbeck / pixelio.de

More available books at **www.hansebooks.com**

1874.

LEHIGH VALLEY RAILROAD.

Tourist's Guide

TO SUMMER RESORTS.

CHICAGO, ROCK ISLAND & PACIFIC RAILWAY.

PASSENGER STATION, CHICAGO.

THE BEST ROUTE
FOR
Leavenworth, Atchison, Topeka, Denver,
AND ALL POINTS IN
KANSAS AND NEW MEXICO.

THE
CONNECTING LINK OF PACIFIC RAILWAY
TO ALL POINTS IN
NEBRASKA, COLORADO, UTAH, CALIFORNIA, AND OREGON.
THE GREAT PACIFIC MAIL ROUTE

BAGGAGE CHECKED TO DESTINATION.

A. M. SMITH, Gen'l Pass'r Agent.   HUGH RIDDLE, Gen'l Sup't.

SPENCER HOUSE,
NIAGARA FALLS.

This Hotel, which is open the year round, and which has been in successful operation since 1867, invites the continued patronage of the pleasure-seeking community.

With the recurrence of each season, its proprietor, in view of its increasing popularity, adopts every improvement and convenience that experience may suggest and the comfort of its guests may seem to require.

ITS PROXIMITY TO THE FALLS
makes it desirable for the Tourist, and
ITS CONVENIENCE TO THE DEPOT
subjects the traveler to no expense for Omnibus or Carriage hire. In conformity with the times, the

PRICES HAVE BEEN REDUCED TO $3.50 A DAY.

The proprietor PLEDGES HIS PERSONAL ATTENTION to his guests, and respectfully solicits a share of the patronage of the traveling public.

A. CLUCK,
Proprietor.

Niagara Falls, June 1st, 1874.

Chicago & North-Western Railway.

THE ROUTE DIRECT

From CHICAGO to OMAHA,   From CHICAGO to GREEN BAY,
From CHICAGO to MILWAUKEE,   From CHICAGO to MARQUETTE,
From CHICAGO to ST. PAUL,   From CHICAGO to SIOUX CITY,
From CHICAGO to MADISON,   From CHICAGO to YANKTON, DAK.,
From CHICAGO to DUBUQUE,

IS VIA THE

CHICAGO & NORTH-WESTERN RAILWAY.

On the arrival of the trains from the East or South, the trains of the Chicago & North-Western Railway leave Chicago as follows:—

For Council Bluffs, Omaha, and California,
Two through trains daily.

For St. Paul and Minneapolis,
Two through trains daily.

For Green Bay and Lake Superior,
Two through trains daily.

For Milwaukee,
Four through trains daily.

For Winona, and points in Minnesota,
One through train daily.

For Dubuque, via Freeport,
Two through trains daily.

For Dubuque and La Crosse, via Clinton,
Two trains daily, each way.

For Sioux City and Yankton,
Two through trains daily.

For Geneva Lake,
Two through trains daily.

For Rockford, Kenosha, Sterling, Janesville, and other local points,
Can have from two to ten express trains daily.

Passenger Fares by this route are always as low as they are by any other.

See that your tickets read "via CHICAGO & NORTH-WESTERN RAILWAY."
This is the Pioneer Route to and from CALIFORNIA AND THE PACIFIC SLOPE.

Tickets over this route are sold by all Ticket Agents in all Coupon Ticket Offices in the United States and the Canadas.

MARVIN HUGHITT, Gen'l Sup't.   W. H. STENNETT, Gen'l Pass'r Agt.

MONTREAL.

C. S. BROWN, J. Q. PERLEY,
PROPRIETORS.

The present proprietors having taken a long lease of this well-known FIRST-CLASS HOTEL, intend using every endeavor to maintain the favorable reputation which it has gained under the present management. Having made large additions to the House, they are now better prepared than ever before for the reception and accommodation of their friends.

MONTREAL TELEGRAPH OFFICE IN THE HOUSE.

TOLEDO, WABASH & WESTERN
RAILWAY.

THE FAST LINE to the WEST.

CLOSE CONNECTIONS WITH EASTERN LINES, AS UNDER:

At TOLEDO with Lake Shore & Michigan Southern Railway.
At FORT WAYNE with Pittsburg & Fort Wayne Railway.
At DANVILLE with I., C. & L. and I., B. & W. Line.

Forming the Leading Thoroughfare to the following Western Points:

FORT WAYNE, LAFAYETTE, DECATUR, PEORIA, {ST. LOUIS} BLOOMINGTON, TOLONO, SPRINGFIELD, JACKSONVILLE,

HANNIBAL, QUINCY, KEOKUK, OTTUMWA,

SEDALIA, LEAVENWORTH, LAWRENCE, {KANSAS CITY} TOPEKA, FORT SCOTT, DENISON,

ST. JOSEPH, ATCHISON,

HOUSTON, LINCOLN, SACRAMENTO, {DENVER} GALVESTON, OMAHA, SAN FRANCISCO.

☞ All trains of the "Great Wabash Route" run through to the Mississippi River *without change*, connecting closely, at St. Louis, Hannibal, Quincy, and Keokuk, with Western Lines for all points in Iowa, Missouri, Kansas, Texas, Colorado, and California.

This is the ONLY ROUTE running Two Daily Lines of PULLMAN PALACE SLEEPING CARS from Cleveland and Toledo to St. Louis, *without change*, and PALACE DAY CARS to Quincy and Kansas City direct.

Secure Tickets via this Great Continuous Thoroughfare, and thereby avoid the trouble and annoyance of Omnibus Transfers and Changing Cars. Tickets for sale at all Ticket Offices in the East, and at the Company's Office, 263 Broadway, New York.

W. L. MALCOLM,
General Passenger Agent, Toledo.

ST. LOUIS HOTEL,

St. Louis Street, Quebec.

This Hotel, which is unrivaled for SIZE, STYLE, and LOCALITY, in Quebec, is open throughout the year for Pleasure and Business Travel.

It is eligibly situated near to, and surrounded by, the most delightful and fashionable promenades—the Governor's Garden, the Citadel, the Esplanade, the Place d'Armes, and Durham Terrace—which furnish the splendid views and magnificent scenery for which Quebec is so justly celebrated, and which is unsurpassed in any part of the world.

The proprietors, in returning thanks for the very liberal patronage they have hitherto enjoyed, inform the public that this Hotel has been THOROUGHLY RENOVATED AND EMBELLISHED, *and can now accommodate about 500 visitors;* and assure them that nothing will be wanting on their part that will conduce to the comfort and enjoyment of their guests.

W. RUSSELL & SON,
Proprietors.

HUDSON RIVER
BY
DAYLIGHT.

JUNE 1st to about OCTOBER 10th,

DAY LINE OF STEAMBOATS
"C. VIBBARD"
AND
"DANIEL DREW."

Leaving New York every morning, except Sunday, from Vestry Street Pier.

TIME TABLE.

GOING NORTH.		GOING SOUTH.	
NEW YORK (Vestry Street)..	8.30 A. M.	ALBANY	8.30 A. M.
" (23d Street)......	8.45 "	Hudson	10.40 "
Yonkers	9.30 "	Catskill	11.00 "
Tarrytown (by ferry-boat)...	10.10 "	Rhinebeck	12.20 P. M.
Nyack " " ...	10.10 "	Poughkeepsie............	1.15 "
West Point...................	11.30 "	Newburg..................	2.10 "
Cornwall......................	11.55 "	Cornwall	2.25 "
Newburg......................	12.10 P. M.	West Point................	2.45 "
Poughkeepsie................	1.10 "	Tarrytown (by ferry-boat)...	4.05 "
Rhinebeck	2.00 "	Nyack " " ...	4.05 "
Catskill........................	3.20 "	Yonkers	4.40 "
Hudson	3.40 "	NEW YORK (23d Street)......	5.35 "
ALBANY.......................	6.00 "	" (Vestry Street)..	5.50 "

Affording the best mode of enjoying the unsurpassed scenery, and of reaching the "Overlook" and "Catskill" Mountain Houses, Lebanon Springs (via Hudson), Sharon Springs, by special train via Susquehanna Railway (all rail from Albany), Saratoga Springs, and all points North and West.

ISAAC L. WELSH,
General Ticket Agent.

KANSAS, COLORADO, AND CALIFORNIA,

VIA THE

St. Louis, Kansas City & Northern
RAILWAY.

THE GREAT THROUGH LINE

FROM ST. LOUIS TO

KANSAS CITY, OMAHA, SAN FRANCISCO, DENVER,

THE BUFFALO RANGES OF KANSAS,

AND

The Health-giving Mountains, Parks, and Plains of Colorado.

Pure Air! Sublime Scenery! Charming Landscapes!

TIME FROM ST. LOUIS TO DENVER,

ONLY 46 HOURS!

Daily Rail and Stage Lines from Denver to Golden City, Central City, Georgetown, Colorado Springs, Idaho Springs, Garden of the Gods, and all points of interest to the pleasure-seeker.

PULLMAN'S PALACE CARS

From St. Louis and Chicago to Kansas City, Kansas City to Denver, and from St. Louis to Omaha, without change.

Tickets for sale at all Offices of the Erie Railway.

W. C. VAN HORNE,　　　　　　　　　　　　　　**P. B. GROAT,**
General Superintendent.　　　　　　　　　　*General Ticket Agent.*

CHICAGO, MILWAUKEE & ST. PAUL
RAILWAY.

THE SHORTEST AND BEST ROUTE
FROM
CHICAGO TO MILWAUKEE

La Crosse, Winona, Lake City,
ST. PAUL, AND MINNEAPOLIS.

The Lines of this Company pass through more leading business centres and attractive pleasure resorts than any other North-western line.

This is the only *through* Route to the North-west, via Chicago, Milwaukee, and the shore of the Upper Mississippi River.

PALACE COACHES AND SLEEPING CARS THROUGH WITHOUT CHANGE.

TRAINS LEAVE CHICAGO from Union Depot, corner Canal and West Madison Streets.

GET TICKETS VIA THIS LINE FROM CHICAGO
DIRECT,

as no Through Tickets, *via Chicago*, Westward, will be received at any other point on this Company's Line after May 1st, 1873.

A. V. H. CARPENTER,	S. S. MERRILL.	JNO. C. GAULT,
Gen'l Passenger and Ticket Agent.	General Manager.	Ass't General Manager.

SUMMER EXCURSIONS

FOR

VIA THE

LEHIGH VALLEY
RAILROAD.

EMBRACING A DESCRIPTION OF THE PICTURESQUE REGIONS, APTLY TERMED

"The Switzerland of America,"

TRAVERSED BY THIS LINE; A BRIEF SKETCH OF EACH POINT OF HISTORICAL OR CONTEMPORANEOUS IMPORTANCE THROUGH WHICH IT PASSES; AND
AN OFFICIAL LIST OF THE

ROUTES AND RATES OF FARE

FOR A SERIES OF

DELIGHTFUL SUMMER EXCURSIONS.

"Fair Pennsylvania! than thy midland vales
Lying 'twixt hills of green, and bound afar
By billowy mountains rolling in the blue,
No lovelier landscape meets the traveler's eye."
— *T. Buchanan Read.*

PHILADELPHIA:
N. VAN HORN, PUBLISHER,
1874.

George M. Colburn,
John H. McOmber, } *Proprietors.*

THIS Hotel, which for many years has enjoyed an enviable reputation for beauty of location, healthfulness of surroundings, strict attention to the wants and close application to the interests of its guests, and for all that constitutes a *strictly first-class place of resort*, has been refurnished and put in complete order in anticipation of a continuance and increase of the liberal patronage which has in the past been bestowed on its present managers.

THE CLIFTON HOUSE

BEING NEARER THE FALLS THAN ANY OTHER HOTEL, AND THE ONLY HOTEL FROM THE PARLORS AND BALCONIES OF WHICH A FULL AND UNINTERRUPTED VIEW OF THE RAPIDS AND FALLS MAY BE OBTAINED,

is thus rendered at once the most convenient and most desirable resort for Pleasure-seekers and Tourists at Niagara. The terms for Board are

THREE DOLLARS AND FIFTY CENTS PER DAY,
(UNITED STATES FUNDS,)

being much less than prices on American side—a fact which alone commends the CLIFTON to public attention. For families who desire to remain by the month or season, special arrangements will be made and liberal inducements offered.

Connected with the CLIFTON are cottages, built expressly to accommodate families who prefer the quiet of a home to the excitement of active hotel life. There are also connected with this Hotel

A SPACIOUS LAWN AND A PLAY-GROUND

for children well shaded with trees and lighted at night with gas. On the premises are

BOWLIN-GALLEYS, BILLIARD-ROOMS, &c.

A SUPERIOR BAND OF MUSIC will be in attendance during the season to enliven the Lawn and Ball-room.

☞Passengers for the CLIFTON who may arrive at the Falls by either the Erie or New York Central Railways, will always find at the Station our porters and stages to convey them to the hotel—a ten minutes ride.

Parties wishing further information, rooms, or rates of board, will please address:

COLBURN & McOMBER,
Niagara Falls, N. Y.

SUMMER EXCURSIONS.

NOT more regularly does the warm summer season recur, than, to the American public, does the desire, begotten of it, to get away from home; to throw everything aside, if only for a day or two, and go off somewhere. And what a blessed comfort it is to shake off the dust of the city, to leave behind and forget for the nonce its hot pavements and dusty walls, and hurry away to some of the cool, leafy nooks nestling somewhere far away among the mountains, or on the shore of some one of the many inland lakes which, like jewels, bestud our northern landscape. In the cold, bleak days of winter we cling instinctively to the family fireside and the indoor delights of our city homes; and naturally enough,—for the winter hearth tells of all that is beautiful and sacred in domestic life; but with the warm breezes wafted by the opening summer's days there comes an inward longing to be off, a desire for a change of scene, a yearning for that abandon, that *dolce far niente*, which can only be found in nature's more secluded haunts.

And, year by year, we Americans are indeed coming to be more and more a summer pleasure-seeking people. The increasing facilities for travel, the establishment of numerous attractive resorts at every point where nature has offered a mingling of the accessible and the picturesque, and the enhanced appreciation of the value of an annual period of relaxation in the popular mind, all these have combined of late years to send everybody off on some sort of a summer trip, from the school-teacher or clerk, with their simple visit of a week to some quiet rural abode, to the luxurious millionaire taking his wife and six handsome daughters, with their dozen Saratoga trunks, for an all-summer's round of Mauch Chunk, Watkins' Glen, Niagara Falls, and the upper St. Lawrence.

And so it is, that when the breath of June steals in through the casement, the clerk jumps down from his high stool, the teacher closes her books, the editor throws down his quill, the merchant forgets his ledger, the clergyman asks for his vacation, the lawyer grows weary of the court-room, and each, packing up his or her valise, draws a long breath, heaves a sigh,—the pent-up feelings of a long winter's toil,—and exclaims, in a tone that admits of no doubt or denial, " I *must* go on a summer excursion somewhere."

And so they must. But then there comes up, first of all, that all-important and, it must be confessed, very pertinent inquiry—

WHERE SHALL I GO?

And this is the question which, so far at least as Philadelphians are concerned, this little work proposes briefly to answer. For, to use the words of Pennsylvania's lamented poet, from whom we have already quoted on the title-page,

"No lovelier landscape meets the traveler's eye"

than that which constitutes the domain of the Keystone State. Tourists travel far and at great expense to reach the mountain-darkened current of the historic Rhine, or to view from the peaks of the Sierra Nevadas the glorious scenery of the plains and the Pacific coast. Yet beauties which equal these, aye, it may be even surpass them, are here within our very borders, and within a few hours' ride of our homes. What mountain scenery can be grander than that in which the silvery Lehigh winds its way through overshadowing hills, now meeting with some apparently impenetrable barrier to its course, or now darting off obliquely to seek the passage-way cleft for it through these rocky battlements by some gigantic convulsion of the past? Here in the torrid days of summer, when city folks swelter and inwardly long for the wings of a bird that they may fly away and be at rest, how many cool, delicious spots there are, free alike from the turmoil of the town and the discomforts of daily routine at home. Come, let us visit some of them. Other sections may boast their charm and attractiveness, and entreat you with the alluring voice of the siren to visit them; but none, no, not one, can show such picturesque beauty, such wild, romantic splendor, such a wealth of nature in her freshest forms, as can the Switzerland of America, the region of Pennsylvania traversed by the Lehigh Valley Road.

But come, take your valise and let us be off. We shall take the morning train on THE NORTH PENNSYLVANIA RAILROAD, from Berks street depot, and by noon-time shall be far away up in the heart of the coal regions. Here, this is our train; jump aboard, and let us select good seats, in one of the luxurious drawing-room coaches by all means. These wheeled palaces in which we now seat ourselves run through to Elmira, and in them—thanks to the enterprise of the Pennsylvania and New York Drawing-room Coach Company—we may accomplish our journey without any of the usual discomforts of travel. There, we hadn't much time to lose, for we are off, you see, already. Leaving the depot we traverse the northern section of the city about a mile east of the old York road, pass, in turn, Fort Washington and the picturesque scenes of Wissahickon, and not until we have ridden seven miles find ourselves without the corporate limits of Philadelphia. Next we reach the neat, pretty Welsh settlements, Penllyn and Gwynedd, the latter having a population of about two thousand. The tunnel through which we pass near this point is a very extensive and costly one, a single mile having cost over $300,000.

At Lansdale, three or four miles further on, we pass the junction point of the branch railroad to Doylestown, the county seat of Bucks county, ten miles distant; and at Sellersville, ten miles further still, reach Landis Ridge, dividing the waters of the Delaware and Schuylkill. A magnificent view of Limestone Valley and Quakertown may be had from the summit of the Ridge, about a mile west of the station. But beauties grander than this are in store for us further on, and we whiz past the stations at Coopersburg, Center Valley, and Bingen, glance for a moment as we pass at Hellertown,—built in 1756 on the site of the old Moravian farms, yet now boasting a population of upwards of six thousand, principally engaged in iron and zinc mining,—and in a few moments more catch glorious glimpses of the majestic hills skirting the valley of the Lehigh, and among which we are shortly to thread our devious way. Now we approach them nearer and nearer, and presently the towering walls of Lehigh University give us notice of our approach to South Bethlehem. Then the houses and spires and chimneys grow more numerous, the silvery Lehigh may be seen plashing at our feet, and almost ere we know it we find ourselves at a stand still at the depot at

BETHLEHEM.

Here it is that we reach the Lehigh Valley Railroad, and a quaint old spot it is, one in which the tourist can well and profitably pass a day or two, in rambling through its quiet streets, so suggestive of days gone by. Here it was that, in 1741, Count Zinzendorf, with his little band of pious Moravians, founded a settlement, and established institutions of learning for both sexes, which in all subsequent generations have attracted pupils hither from all parts of the country, and which to-day are inferior to none in the land. These seminaries, together with the Lehigh University, before mentioned, combine to give Bethlehem a justly-earned reputation as an educational centre. The University, which was inaugurated in 1866, was founded by the liberality of Hon. Asa Packer, who gave not only the fifty-six acres upon which it stands, but the princely sum of half a million dollars besides. A visit to the institution, with its stately edifices and its beautiful forest park, will amply repay the tourist. So, too, will a stroll through the city, where will be found remaining most of the old Moravian buildings, all of stone, and quaint in their architecture. The principal ones, which stand at the foot of Broad street, were used as a hospital by General Washington, when his troops retreated across the Delaware, and it was here too that the Moravian nuns gave Count Pulaski the banner still preserved by the Baltimore Historical Society, the presentation of which gave Longfellow occasion for that beautiful, familiar poem, beginning

"Take thy banner, may it wave
Lightly o'er the good and brave."

But it is not in antiquities alone that Bethlehem possesses an interest. In modern progress and improvements, too, does she put in her claims to attention. Her foundries, mills, and factories are varied and extensive. She has four banks, fifteen churches, two public halls, many handsome private residences, and a population of nearly ten thousand. Many pleasant drives and views are to be had in the environs, and a visit to Nisky Hill, overlooking the town, discloses one of the most tastefully laid out cemeteries in the country.

So, altogether, Bethlehem is a point we could scarce afford to miss on our tour. But the whistle is blowing, and our train will soon be starting off on its trip up the valley. But, wait! No—that is the train just coming in from New York to connect with our own—for it is at this point that the streams of excursion travel from the two great cities of America—New York and Philadelphia—coalesce and become one. There is the New York train now; its passengers left the metropolis this morning, and here they are ready to go on with us up the valley.

FROM NEW YORK TO BETHLEHÉM

is, indeed, a delightful ride. Leaving New York by the Central Railroad of New Jersey from the foot of Liberty street, or by the Morris and Essex Railroad from the foot of Barclay street, the tourist traverses the most fertile farming regions of New Jersey, skirts the mountain range which overlooks the fair valley of the Musconetcong, and finally reaches the Delaware, at Phillipsburg, directly opposite the flourishing city of Easton. This is the terminus of the Lehigh Valley Railroad, —and, crossing the river on a bridge affording an unequaled view of the city and the confluent rivers which border it, the traveler soon finds himself, without change of coaches, whizzing along up the south bank of the Lehigh, past Glendon, Redington, and Freemansburg, to the great junction point with the line of travel from Philadelphia at Bethlehem.

And thus it is, then, that our fellow-passengers from New York find themselves here, ready to go on with us, and explore the beauties of the far-famed valley above. And now we are off, and Bethlehem is soon behind us. Take your seat, for the present, at all events, on the right hand, or river side, of the car, and you will see much to entertain you in the view of immense blast furnaces, long rows of canal boats in the canal opposite, sleepy farm-houses nestling here and there

BETHLEHEM.

among the hills on the opposite side, pretty-shaded islands in the river, and everywhere, if in summer, a luxuriance of foliage and flowers. At East Penn Junction our train connects for Reading, Harrisburg, and Pittsburg, but that is not the direction in which we are going to-day. " Young man, go north-west," is the motto for this occasion. Next we come to the populous city of

ALLENTOWN,

Named after an old friend of William Penn, and founded in 1762. It is situated at the junction of Little Lehigh and Jordan Creeks with the Lehigh River, and is regularly and tastefully laid out with broad, clean, and well-shaded streets, and a fine public square in its centre, while the presence of gas-lamps, hydrants, and horse-cars gives it an unmistakably metropolitan air. It has a population of about fifteen thousand. Here, too, we find—in the stone bridge, eighteen hundred feet long, spanning Jordan Creek by nineteen arches—the largest structure of the kind in the State. Among its industries Allentown boasts several rolling-mills and iron-works, woolen and planing mills, carriage, planing, and sash factories, and a host of similar minor establishments. It has also three national banks, a handsome court-house and jail, three costly public school-houses, eighteen churches, nearly a dozen newspapers, Odd Fellows' and Masonic halls, a fine opera-house, and numerous other showy public edifices. The fair grounds, covering twelve acres, in the outskirts of the city, contain a fine exhibition building, known as Floral Hall, a race-track, and stalls for one hundred head of horses and cattle. Among the private educational establishments Muhlenburg College, founded in 1848, and the Allentown Female College are prominent. The scenery and natural curiosities of the city and vicinity are well worth seeing. There are several romantic springs near by, much resorted to by strangers, and from Bauer's Rock, close at hand, one may look down from an elevation of a thousand feet upon the rich and varied landscapes of the Saucon and Lehigh Valleys.

CATASAUQUA,

Three miles beyond Allentown, signifies ' parched land," and takes its name from a creek here flowing into the Lehigh. It was here that anthracite iron was first made in the Lehigh Valley, and now the town turns out twenty-five thousand car-wheels annually. Founded in 1839 by Philadelphians, it was in 1853 incorporated, and to-day has a population of six thousand; is supplied with gas and water, has twelve public schools, eleven churches, two papers, a bank, and a fine public or town hall. The railroad to Fogelsville, twenty miles distant, diverges at this point from our line.

Just beyond Catasauqua stands a stone building nearly two centuries old, once occupied by George Taylor, one of the signers of the Declaration of Independence. More than once, too, its now crumbling walls have afforded the earlier settlers a place of refuge and defense against attack by the wily Indian.

Another mile brings us to the thriving village of

HOKENDAUQUA,

Also named after a neighboring creek, and signifying *searching for land*. Though not twenty years settled, it has a population of twelve hundred, and an extensive iron-works, the amount of labor done in which may be estimated from the simple sta ement that it consumes one hundred thousand tons of coal annually.

COPLAY,

The town which we next pass, is the site of the Lehigh Valley Iron Works, and the mills of the Coplay Cement Company. At

WHITEHALL,

Deriving its name from that of the adjacent country residence of a Philadelphia gentlemen, stood the antiquated place of worship known as Egypt Church, originally built in 1742, again in 1785, and finally, in 1851, replaced by a more modern structure. In 1763 this locality was the scene of many Indian tragedies. Passing in turn Laury, with its slate quarries, and Rockdale, with its precipitous cliffs, along whose giddy brink our train glides in seeming mockery of danger, we reach

SLATINGTON,

The centre, as its name indicates, of an extensive slate business. Many a dunce in schools in every part of the land has wept away over the figures of some incomprehensible sum in arithmetic, scrawled in school-boy figures, over the productions of this vicinity. The capitol at Washington is roofed with slate from this point. Trout Creek runs directly through Slatington, which, indeed, is a place of some importance, boasting twenty-five hundred inhabitants, four or five churches, and a weekly paper. There are also some important slate quarries at Slatedale, three and one-half miles distant, and connected by a branch road with the main line. And now, as we resume our ride, there presently breaks upon us a scene of surpassing beauty, none other than the famous

LEHIGH GAP,

Through which the river forces its irresistible way through the rocky barriers of the Blue Ridge. To the traveler who has not seen this grand commingling of nature's forces, no words can suffice to describe its sublimity or beauty. On the

LEHIGH GAP.

western side, near the summit of a lofty ridge, stands out abrupt and lone a gray, towering crag, surmounted by a tuft of withered pines, and known as the " Devil's Pulpit." The scene is strangely wild and weird, and involuntarily recalls the days when these solitudes had not yet re-echoed to the invading footsteps of man :

> " Or here, perchance,
> In desperate hour, some Indian maid forlorn
> Hath to the midnight flung her streaming hair—
> Plunged, like the Pleiad, to be seen no more."

A stop for a day or two at this charming and picturesque point will amply repay the lover of nature. The view given herewith conveys some idea of its beauty to the reader. But the knowing ones will tell you that there are even grander beauties beyond. Now we see busy Parryville, then Weissport and

LEHIGHTON,

A town sixty years old, and containing fifteen hundred inhabitants and four church societies. Near it are a mineral spring, quite famous for its healing properties, and the grounds of the Carbon County Agricultural Society.

This vicinity teems, too, in vivid historical reminiscences and traditions. The survivors of the Wyoming massacre called a portion of it the "Shades of Death," so lonely were its solitudes and fastnesses. Here, in 1746, settled Moravian missionaries, preaching to the Indians their gospel of peace, and, for a while, successfully. But ten years later, during the hostilities which followed Braddock's defeat, the savages committed bloody excesses hereabout, and even as late as 1780 carried off a white family hence to Canada. In Weissport, it may be added, is the site of a log hut built and occupied by Benjamin Franklin while in charge of the then north-western frontier. At

PACKERTON

We cross the river and see the extensive shops of the Lehigh Valley Railroad Company, employing nearly six hundred men, and close at hand, too, is a park of seventy-five acres stocked with elk, deer, and antelopes. Brook-trout breeding is also extensively and successfully carried on near by.

But, as we are looking and wondering, a sudden turn in the valley brings us in full view of

MAUCH CHUNK.

Alighting for the first time in this picturesque spot, where the enterprise of man has engirded with railroads and canals the wildest mountain solitude, one knows not whether first to bow in awe at nature's majesy, or exclaim with delight at the triumph which engineering skill has achieved in rendering it so easily accessible to the outer world; for this narrow gorge, through which the Lehigh through ages of solitude plashed its way to the sea, now furnishes an avenue also for two railroads, a canal, and at this point a village street, all crowded into this narrow space, and monopolizing every inch of room they can ever expect to occupy.

MAUCH CHUNK.

The place derives its name, Mauch Chunk, signifying Bear Mountain, from this cone-like elevation on our right, under the shadow of which stands the tasteful depot at which we alight. From this point we cross first the canal and then the river by a bridge of two spans and find ourselves before the Mansion House, (see advertisement published elsewhere,) on the principal street of the town.

First, let us take a seat here on the cosy veranda of the hotel, and take our bearings. That gigantic mountain south of us, turning abruptly to the eastward, with the carriage road ascending along its rugged slope, is known as the Flagstaff; and from Prospect Rock, which may be reached by a rustic foot-path from the hotel grounds, there is to be had a glorious view of the river and the valley, both far below. Looking in the opposite direction the eye follows the narrow highway, first with its single row of buildings facing the river, and then built up on both sides to the foot of Mount Pisgah, an almost perpendicular elevation rising to the height of fifteen hundred feet above the tide-water, and about the base of which cluster, in what seems at first a hopeless confusion, the dwellings, stores, and churches of this active little town. It is over Mount Pisgah that by-and-by we shall enjoy a ride on the famous gravity railroad known as the "Switchback." For the present, however, a few words about the history of the locality itself. Though first settled only in the year 1815, it was in this immediate vicinity that about a quarter of a century earlier (1791) anthracite coal was accidentally discovered by one Philip Ginter, a hunter. Upon the strength of this, the Lehigh Coal Mine Company was formed in the following year, but it was not until the war of 1812 had begun that the company prosecuted mining with any activity, and finally, in 1815, the organization disbanded. Three years later, however, the Lehigh Navigation and the Lehigh Coal Companies were formed, and out of their subsequent consolidation grew the present Lehigh Coal and Navigation Company, whose shipments sometimes of late years have amounted to eighteen thousand tons weekly. Gradually, with the development of its mining interests, Mauch Chunk has grown to a place of six thousand five hundred inhabitants, and is moreover, from its natural beauty of scenery and surroundings, annually becoming more popular as a summer resort. It has three weekly newspapers, two banks, nine churches, a public library, good schools, and a number of elegant residences, among which those of the Hon. Asa Packer and of Mr. Leisenring are especially noticeable.

"THE SWITCHBACK."

The first problem presented for solution by the Lehigh Coal and Navigation Company when organized, was the transportation of coal from the mines to the river. Science and enterprise joined hands to solve it. First, a tedious system of mule teams was adopted, but in 1827 this was replaced by the gravity railroad, running on a descending grade from Summit Hill to the river. Cars coming down on this road by their own gravity carried with them the mules which were to drag them back. In 1844 the mule system was abandoned entirely, by the erection of inclined planes and stationary engines. Since that time, a ride over these planes has annually become more popular, until now it is an inseparable feature of a visit to Mauch Chunk.

But let us step into this car which is waiting here at the base of the plane, and we shall shortly see how it is for ourselves. The view, even here at the starting-point at Upper Mauch Chunk, overlooking the town, the river, and East Mauch Chunk, is fine enough to satisfy any reasonable sight-seer. But here we go! up—up—up. Now we begin to look down on the tree-tops, and the landscape below seems to be slowly but steadily receding. We speedily traverse the two thousand three hundred and twenty-two feet of track, and, reaching the summit, are in reality eight hundred and sixty-four feet higher than our starting-point. Passing over a trestle-work, spanning a wild ravine, we alight and follow a winding footpath to a still higher point—the Pavilion, where, from an observatory, we may look down upon a view than which certainly none more grand could be wished for by mortal eye. Away to the south, through Lehigh Gap, we catch glimpses of the hazy blue outline of Schooley's Mountain, sixty-five miles distant. North of it, too, is Wind Gap, and following the horizon around we see a mingled panorama of blue hills and green forests, bewildering in its extent and grandeur. To this fascinating spot have been justly applied the favorite lines from Scott:

        "So wond'rous wild, the whole might seem
        The scenery of a fairy-dream."

And now from this point we whiz along, with gravity for our motive power, for a distance of six miles, (a descent of three hundred and two feet,) to the base of another inclined plane (Mount Jefferson) two thousand and seventy feet long and four hundred and sixty-two feet in elevation. Again we see the earth seeming to recede from us, and again, after reaching the summit, drawn by invisible chargers, we hurry along, over a mile's descent of forty-five feet, to the quaint mining village of Summit Hill, with a population of two thousand, and an elevation of nine hundred and seventy-five feet above the Lehigh. A curious place it is, with rambling streets, old buildings, and a stone arsenal with turrets and loop-holes, and in which are stored arms for a company of militiamen, to be called out should disorders arise among the miners. Close at hand is another, or the original switchback railroad, leading, by a long descent, to the Panther Creek Valley beyond; and here, too, is the "burning mine," within the subterranean depths of which a fiery heat has been raging for thirty-two years past, searing and blighting whole acres on the surface above it.

But the supreme pleasure of our ride is yet in store for us. It is the return over the nine miles of continuous descending grade to our starting point at Mount Pisgah's base. A single turn of the brakes and off we start, faster and faster, down through long stretches of shaded roadway, around wondrous curves, along giddy cliffs, under the shadows of great ivy-grown crags, and still down—down—down, at a dizzy speed, and as if borne on the wings of the wind. There, like a toy village in the distance before, and far below us, we once more descry Mauch Chunk, with its familiar church spire so indelibly impressed upon all who have visited the town. How fast we seem to be approaching it. And so, indeed, we are; for almost ere we know it our fleet charger has drawn rein, and we are safe and sound, but breathless with delight and excitement, at the platform from which we so recently started on our ascent.

It may safely be said that, in all the varied features of American tourist travel, there can be found nothing so novel or exhilarating as a ride over the Switchback; and a visit to Mauch Chunk without it is to a summer tour, what, to the Shakspearean drama, is Hamlet with Hamlet omitted.

But a stay at Mauch Chunk affords still another delight—a visit to

GLEN ONOKO.

A ride of two miles further up the river, by any of the trains, will bring us to it, and a wild-tangled spot we shall find it,—a mountain ravine through which a crystal stream comes plashing down in successive waterfalls from a height of over nine hundred feet. The pathway to the summit leads us along the course of the streamlet—now on this side, now on that, spanning it here and there with a rustic bridge, which it were not difficult to imagine that elfin hands had placed there, and in crossing which we look both forward and backward upon genuine glimpses of fairy-land. The ascent is steep, but will repay us for the toil. There is no royal road to the summit here. We must go afoot, if we go at all, so let us start forward. A few steps from the depot bring us to the foot of a long stairway, and, passing Entrance and Crystal Cascades, we see above us a rustic bridge, upon which our pathway soon brings us. Here we are face to face with Moss Cascade, below us is a limpid pool known as the Lover's Bath, while frowning above, as grim sentinels, are two moss-clad boulders, called the Pulpit Rocks, each about twenty feet high. Next we pass by the Laurel Cascade, to what is aptly termed the Heart of the Glen, where, amid a dense luxuriance of foliage, the eye rests upon a series of minor falls, called the Stairway Cascades, leaping in playful rivalry one upon the other. From this point a stairway ingeniously hewn out from the trunk of a monster hemlock leads us to Sunrise Point, from which may be obtained a glorious and commanding view of the landscape of the winding valley now far, far below. But we cannot pause long here, for before us is one of the greatest charms of the glen, Chameleon Falls, fifty feet high, over which the stream plunges into a half-square basin, densely overshadowed with foliage.

CHAMELEON FALLS.

And not far above it, too, we come to Onoko Falls, the highest, and in the opinion of many, the handsomest in the glen. If we have the courage to venture behind this misty veil of ninety feet in height, we shall obtain a glimpse of sprite land which will well repay us for the chance of a slight ducking from the spray.

ONOKO FALLS.

Resuming our upward journey, and having previously squeezed through between two birch trees by a passage-way justly named the Fat Man's Misery, we pass, in turn, Terrace Cascade and Cave Falls, the latter deriving its name from a neighboring rocky recess in which the Indians are said to have frequently concealed themselves. Indeed, through this glen ran an old war-trail from the Susquehanna to the Delaware, and it was by this route that General Sullivan and his soldiers passed in 1778, after the Wyoming massacre. Next, our path leads us by a deserted old cabin, a convenient halting-place for sportsmen, to Packer's Point, where, amid an extended view of the surrounding country, we have reached the summit of Glen Onoko's beauties.

TERRACE FALLS.

And now, once more resuming our journey, we find our way, as before, following the devious windings of the Lehigh amid scenery so wild and lonely as to recall the descriptions we have read in childhood of the mysterious Black Forest and Hartz Mountains of Germany. The hills, some of them seven hundred feet high, descend abruptly to the very edge of the hemlock-dyed waters rushing rapidly by them in a thousand plashes and eddies, and along wondrously cut ledges near their base we whirl onward, in perfect security, in our palatial coaches. Our first stopping-place in these wilds is

PENN HAVEN JUNCTION,

from which diverge three important branches, known as the Beaver Meadow, Hazleton, and Mahanoy Divisions, each of them connecting with important coal centres, distant respectively sixty-six, seventy, and eighty-one miles. Penn Haven itself was founded in 1838, and now does an immense coal business.

VIEW ON STONY CREEK.

STONY CREEK

derives its name from a romantic trout-stream in its immediate vicinity, a favorite resort of sportsmen and picnic parties.

ROCKPORT

Is a village situated in a picturesque gorge in Buck Mountain, on the opposite side of the river from the station bearing its name. At this point may be obtained especially noticeable evidence of the disastrous freshet of 1862, which laid the whole valley temporarily in ruins. Passing Tannery, a lumber station, with its little collection of six hundred inhabitants, we come next to

WHITE HAVEN,

Named from Josiah White, the enterprising founder of the Lehigh Coal and Navigation Company. Before the railroad came, packets ran on the canal between this point, Mauch Chunk and Easton, and even to-day such a mode of conveyance through this glorious scenery would not be without its attractions, perhaps. The town has fifteen hundred inhabitants, six churches, and a savings bank. In the freshet of 1862 it was a conspicuous sufferer, sustaining a loss of one hundred and fifty lives, and property valued at two and a half million dollars. Some idea of the peril of the situation may be formed from the statement that the river rose thirty feet above low-water mark, and that, too, in some places at the rate of nine feet in five minutes.

At White Haven our Niagara Falls express train stops for twenty minutes, enabling hungry passengers to regale themselves with a good old-fashioned country dinner, and prepare thus for a keener enjoyment of the beautiful scenery beyond.

Passing Moosehead, where there is an extensive ochre factory, we next reach Fairview, where, crossing the track of the Lehigh and Susquehanna, we find ourselves at the summit of the mountain, and, looking down, catch our first glimpse of the romantic and storied Valley of Wyoming.

BUY THE TRAVELERS' OFFICIAL GUIDE
Of the Railways and Steam Navigation Lines in the United States and Canada. The only Guide recognized by the General Ticket and Passenger Agents' Association. Adopted by the United States Government as the standard of the Quartermaster and Post Office Departments. For sale on all trains and at news stands. **Subscription price, $3.00 per annum; single copies, 40 cents.**

BUY THE GAZETTEER OF RAILWAY STATIONS
IN THE UNITED STATES AND THE DOMINION OF CANADA.
It designates telegraph, express, post, and money-order offices, and gives the population of the several places; also, contains a list of the counties, county towns, and time of holding courts in the several States, together with much other valuable information. For sale at bookstores and at news stands. **Price, in paper, $1.00 per copy; in cloth, $1.50.**

Send orders to
W. F. ALLEN,
Business Manager National Railway Publication Co., 233 South Fifth St., Philadelphia, Pa.

FIRST GLIMPSE OF THE WYOMING VALLEY.

NEWPORT.

And what a spectacle is this which meets our admiring gaze! To see it were well worth a journey ten times that we have taken. It is simply indescribably grand. For a distance of twenty miles we may follow the winding course of the

Susquehanna—now gleaming in the green meadow land, now losing itself among the mountains, and now reappearing beyond them. Hereabouts we have an area of forty thousand acres, dotted with towns and hamlets, and teeming with life and activity. Before us is the scene of the terrible Avondale disaster of 1869, south of it is Nanticoke, and in the opposite direction is our next place of destination—Wilkesbarre.

But before we reach it, a few words concerning the history of this charming vale in which it stands. It was an old Indian battle-ground often contested by the red men; but in 1769 a company of forty adventurous colonists from Connecticut (where won't those Yankees go?) set up a stockade and claimed possession. They were opposed by a prior claim from some Pennsylvania settlers, and the result was a war which was only ended by the necessity of a common defense during the Revolution. For in 1778 the British sent a force of seven hundred Iroquois and four hundred Tories, under Col. John Butler, to attack the people of the valley, who, in the absence of most of their able-bodied men with Washington's army, could only muster a force of three hundred men and boys for defense. An engagement on July 3d, 1778, resulted in a victory for the invaders, who followed it up by such a wholesale torture and massacre of their captives, women and children included, as the historian is fortunately seldom called upon to record. A boulder, known as "Queen Esther's Rock," standing near the riverbank, is pointed out as marking the spot where one old Seneca half-breed was allowed to murder twenty bound victims in revenge for the death of her son. The dwellings in the valley were reduced to ashes; those of the inhabitants who could, sought safety in flight; and now a granite obelisk, appropriately inscribed, has been erected upon the battle-field in commemoration of this, the most terrible and bloody episode in the struggle which made our country free, and which, in his "Gertrude of Wyoming," the poet Campbell has rendered famous in song and story.

But as we muse on these tragic memories, we reach, first, South Wilkesbarre, and then the important city of which it is a suburb—

WILKESBARRE.

We find the city beautifully laid out on the east bank of the Susquehanna (North branch), and with a population of about twenty-five thousand. It was laid out originally in 1772, and settled in 1773, by the Susquehanna Land Company of Connecticut, deriving its name conjointly from John Wilkes, of London, and Colonel Barré, a distinguished British officer. Many of the memorable scenes of the Indian war were located within the present city limits, and Fort

Wyoming is said to have stood on the river-bank close to the street of the same name. The city of to-day contains eighteen churches, twenty-one schools, six banks, three street railways, and many fine private and public buildings. The enterprise of the people is also shown in the substantial suspension bridge of wire, six hundred and fifty-eight feet long, spanning the river just below the depot. The suburbs abound in pleasant resorts. Prospect Rock, upon the mountain directly back of the town; Harvey's Lake, a noted fishing-ground about twelve miles to the north-west, and the Wyoming Monument, previously mentioned, should all be visited by tourists to this point.

Nine miles beyond Wilkesbarre we come to

PITTSTON,

At the head of the valley and close to the confluence of the Lackawanna and Susquehanna Rivers. Its population is about seventeen thousand, and its suburb, West Pittston, on the other side of the last-mentioned river, contains about two thousand more. Pittston owes its rapid growth chiefly to the extensive mining operations of the Pennsylvania Coal Company; but in addition to this prominent industry, it has also large iron-works and several factories. The West Branch Canal and three lines of railroad intersect it. In the vicinity is a famous rock known as Campbell's Ledge, so named, some say, from a Mr. Campbell, who leaped therefrom to escape his Indian pursuers.

One mile from Pittston we come to the

LACKAWANNA AND BLOOMSBURG JUNCTION,

Where passengers change cars for Scranton, Bloomsburg, Catawissa, and Northumberland.

RANSOM FALLS, McKUNE'S, AND LA GRANGE,

Which we pass next in the order named, are minor stations, each doing considerable local trade.

TUNKHANNOCK

Is the county seat of Wyoming, and quite an important business centre, with a population of twelve hundred, several churches, a Masonic hall, and a national bank. In this locality considerable blue stone is quarried and shipped to Philadelphia and New York.

VOSBURG

Is chiefly noticeable as being the depot for Washington township. One mile distant from it, in a straight line, but seven miles by our rail route, is

MEHOOPANY,

So called from a neighboring creek. It contains two churches and several mills, and is something of a lumber depot.

MESHOPPEN,

Also named from a creek, is a settlement over a half century old, and possesses three churches, several mills, extensive quarries, and a tannery.

Passing, in turn, Black Walnut and its profitable quarries, Skinner's Eddy, and Laceyville, settled in 1830, our next important stopping-place is

WYALUSING,

Which, in Indian parlance, signifies "beautiful hunting-ground." In the village, half a mile from the river's left bank, and containing about five hundred inhabitants, the Moravians originally settled; but troubles with the savages compelled them to abandon the spot. Subsequently, and after the Wyoming massacre, Colonel Hartley's expedition in search of the murderers reached this point, and, continuing on, were attacked near the village. A monument, fifteen feet high, of stone from Campbell's Ledge, was erected here June 15th, 1871, and can be seen between the railroad and the river as we pass.

FRENCHTOWN

Was, at one time, a place of refuge for many of the French nobility who fled from Paris during the Revolution of 1793. These, in company with some Philadelphians, secured possession of a million acres, incorporating themselves as the Asylum and Holland Land Company, and the descendants of some of them are to-day among the best farmers of this section. Beyond Rummerfield, a ferry-crossing, we come to

STANDING STONE,

So called from a stone, forty feet high, standing upright in the river, opposite the village, and familiar as a landmark as far back as the middle of the last century.

WYSAUKING,

Situated in the centre of a fertile farming country, appropriately signifies "the place of grapes." Here may be seen the model twelve-hundred-acre farm of Colonel Piollet.

And now we cross the river by a handsome bridge of nine spans, measuring one thousand four hundred and eighty-five feet in all, and obtain a fine view of our next stopping-place,

TOWANDA,

The capital of Bradford county, and first settled in 1812. It was originally called Meansville, in honor of its founder, William Means; then Williamston; and finally got its present name from the Indian title of a creek south-east of the town, signifying "at the burial-place,"—the Indians being supposed to have buried their dead there. The town has a population of four thousand, several public halls, a bank, three newspapers, six churches, several schools, and a fine academy, called the Susquehanna Collegiate Institute. Its industries are numerous and varied.

ULSTER,

Formerly called Sheshequin, was once a Moravian mission station.

MILAN

Is chiefly important as the nearest station to a tract called "Queen Esther's Flats," once owned by the royal squaw whose name figures so prominently in the Wyoming massacre.

ATHENS

We find located on the peninsula formed by the junction of the Chemung with the Susquehanna. In 1737 it was the site of the Delaware Indian town Diahoga. In 1783 the white settlers found their way hither, and three years later a grant was issued for a township to be called Athens. In 1831 it was incorporated, and since then its growth has been slow but steady. It has six churches, two newspapers, a bank, and a population of about one thousand. North-west of the town is a bluff, one hundred and seventy-five feet high, rising abruptly from the valley, and called Spanish Hill. Tradition says that ancient fortifications have existed on its summit and Spanish coins been discovered thereon.

Crossing the Chemung we next find ourselves in New York State, on the line of the

ERIE RAILWAY,
AT WAVERLY,

Situated directly on the boundary line dividing the Empire and Keystone States, which line, indeed, passes but a few rods south of the station, and at one point intersects a tavern bar-room so effectually that the barkeeper is in one State and the customer in the other.

The place was incorporated in 1854, and notwithstanding a disastrous fire three years ago, has a population of about five thousand, numerous manufactories, gas-works, four churches, two papers, two banks, and a fine public school system.

CHEMUNG,

The next station, was formerly called Brockville, and is the centre of a great stock-raising and wool-growing region.

WELLSBURG

Is a manufacturing village, with a population of a few hundred. It was in this vicinity that General Sullivan threw up breastworks while pursuing the British and Indians, and subsequently routed the foe in a short but bloody conflict.

And now, still following the beautiful valley of the Chemung, we finally reach our temporary stopping-place,

ELMIRA,

Nestling away amid the shadows of the environing hillsides, and looking for all the world like a huge slice of our own Philadelphia or New York. It was settled in 1788, and now has a population of about twenty thousand. As an emporium of trade or travel, few cities of its size surpass it,—railroads extending from it towards all four points of the compass, and the Chemung Canal here connecting the waters of Seneca Lake with the Chemung River, and thence by the Susquehanna with the sea-coast cities and the Atlantic Ocean. The coal traffic passing through the place is also immense. As might be supposed, with such facilities, the city has grown at a wondrous rate. It is handsomely planned, abounds in churches, schools, and public and private enterprises, and is, in short, a city where even the most fastidious can find both a winter and a summer home. Eldridge Park is one of the attractions which no visitor in Elmira should fail to see and admire.

Here, for a time, we stop, and we could not ask to have our lines cast in pleasanter places. Here is the Rathbun House, E. R. Abbott, proprietor, and here, too, the Hathaway House, S. H. Wadsworth, proprietor, both of which are advertised elsewhere in this work, and at either of which we can find home comforts during our stay.

We shall want, too, to take a run up to WATKINS' GLEN, from Elmira. The visit to the Glen is simply indispensable to the tourist in this section, and, indeed, "no family should be without it." First, however, let us continue on our tour as far as Niagara, take a brief glimpse of the St. Lawrence and points beyond, and then return to find that none of their vaunted charms surpass this romantic little nook, with its modest name of "Watkins' Glen." (For description of Watkins' Glen, see page 30.)

When we resume our journey westward to Niagara Falls from Elmira, it is in the palatial Pullman cars of the Erie express train, and looking out from their broad windows, we catch glimpses of many a varied landscape, beauteous with the agricultural wealth of the Southern Tier. Now we reach Corning, with its eight thousand inhabitants,—here diverges the branch to Avon Springs and Rochester. Then, forty miles farther on, we reach the great junction-point at Hornellsville, where we may stop and procure, if we are hungry, a substantial meal. From this point, the main line of the Erie continues on to Salamanca (where connections are made for Cleveland and Cincinnati) and Dunkirk. We, however, strike off to the right, and head straight for Buffalo. The ride is one of rare beauty. By-and-by we cross the famous Portage Bridge,—said to be the largest trestle-work in the world,—spanning an immense gorge three hundred and eighty feet deep, through which the Genesee River leaps in three successive falls. This grand scenery alone would almost suffice to repay the sight-seer for a journey hither.

Then our course takes us along the mountain slope, overlooking the beauteous town of Warsaw; then we pass Attica; just before reaching Buffalo, switch off again to the right, pass Tonawanda, and suddenly find ourselves within sound of the roaring of

NIAGARA FALLS.

Of course, our first move is to choose a hotel, and there is no lack in this respect, depend upon it. We must stay here two or three days, so let us be comfortable. This season, it is said, unusual efforts are to be made to protect visitors against imposition or extortion of any kind. There are some reasonable landlords and some honest hackmen here, after all, we shall find. First, suppose we cross the river by the new bridge, and a wonderful bridge it is. On the Canada side, we gain a splendid view of the Horseshoe, and may visit, if we choose, the different museums, and have our pictures taken. We shall note, too, what has never before been the case here, that the Provincial Government has this year adopted the strictest police regulations to protect visitors. Returning to the American side and leaving our carriage, we may cross by the frail bridge to Goat and Luna Islands, which overlook the very brink of the watery precipice. These are the main features of the Falls; but there are a thousand minor beauties and oddities which have been so often described that we shall leave them for the reader to use in filling up the chinks in his or her imagination until the time for actually seeing them arrives. But one thing we would advise: while you are at the Falls, see everything that there is to be seen; don't give up to fatigue; see it all while there, and leave nothing unseen, to be regretted after your return home. During your stay you will find the Spencer House or the Clifton House delightful and commodious places of abode. If at any time you are going west from Niagara Falls, the Great Western and Michigan Central Railroad, crossing the Suspension Bridge and running palatial coaches through without change to Detroit and Chicago, will be found the most direct and available route from this point. From Niagara Falls, it is also a short ride to

TORONTO OR LEWISTON,

Where the tourist may take the daily steamers of the Royal Mail Line for that most charming of summer trips—a sail down the St. Lawrence River, past the far-famed Thousand Islands which stud its current, to Montreal, Quebec, to the wilder beauties of the Saguenay, to Lakes Champlain and George, and to the White Mountains. At Montreal, the Ottawa House, and at Quebec, the St. Louis Hotel, offer the finest of accommodations for tourists, while those who visit Lake Champlain will not, of course, fail to stop at Fouquet's famous hotel at Plattsburg. The celebrated Au Sable Chasm is distant only twelve miles from this house, and is reached by a delightful carriage drive along the shore of Lake Champlain, winding through beautiful groves, and fording the Au Sable River just above its mouth, affording a fine opportunity for picnic parties, who are furnished with complete outfits and conveyed from the hotel daily. Through tickets, it may be stated, allow passengers to stop over at this hotel and resume their trip at pleasure. Passing hence, down Lake Champlain, via Lake George and Ticonderoga, and thence over the historic battle-ground of Saratoga to Troy and Albany, the tourist may take one of the splendid steamers of the Day Line at the latter city, and, amid a contemplation of the grand and varied beauties which line the majestic Hudson, including the Catskills and West Point, may find a fitting close to the delightful tour which we have herein briefly and imperfectly sketched.

GLEN CATHEDRAL.

WATKINS' GLEN.

During our stay at Elmira, we promised the reader a run up to Watkins' Glen, nor shall we disappoint him. Taking the cars of the Northern Central Railroad from Elmira, we ride a distance of twenty-two miles, and reach the village of Watkins', nestling in a narrow valley, amid a profusion of shrubbery, at the head of Seneca Lake. A walk or ride of half a mile up the main street, parallel with the mountain slope, brings us to a bridge spanning a shallow stream, which has formed for itself, through the lower slope of the mountain range, a passage-way, which terminates abruptly, at a distance of a few hundred yards, in a lofty wall. This wall, however, recedes so as to form a sort of cavernous recess, from one angle of which the stream issues. Behind this solemn gateway of natural masonry, broken and abraded in places by time and the action of the elements, lie the wonderful ravines, the infinite variety of waterfalls and foaming rapids and deep and silent pools which have become famous within a few years, under the designation of Watkins' Glen. It is not for the beautiful lake, nor for the pleasant village, but to see this remarkable *natural wonder*—Watkins' Glen—that the thousands come. It is but recently that it has been accessible to visitors; ten years ago it was almost unknown; now it is a famous summer resort, visited by thousands annually, and claiming a place among the most noted of American scenery.

The mode of ingress to the Glen is by a succession of strongly-constructed stairways built along the face of the precipice, with occasional platforms, from which the more interesting features can be studied, and narrow footpaths cut in the solid rock, with short, picturesque bridges thrown from projecting points, and all securely guarded by convenient hand-rails.

Once inside the rocky barrier, we cross the chasm by a narrow but secure bridge, commanding a fine view of the first cascade, rushing headlong through a rift in the rocks, and falling, roaring and foaming, into a deep basin hollowed out from the water's constant fretting and chafing upon them. Clambering hence, up a series of steps, we follow the fantastic windings of a narrow footpath cut from the face of the cliff, until suddenly our progress is barred by a transverse wall, over which the waters of the long cascade fall from a great height into the dark pool below. At this point, the ragged and lofty walls of the gorge draw close together, and where the footpath ends, a long staircase, wet with mist and spray, is flung at an angle of ninety degrees across the tremendous chasm, connecting, at its farther end, with another footpath, on a higher level of at least fifty feet. Following this, we come upon a series of cascades, dropping from ledge to ledge, with deep pools and broad shallows intervening. Looking upwards here, a little narrow thread of sky, between the tall, towering cliffs of dark rock which shut us in, alone reminds us of the outer world. The air is cool and fresh, and laden with the fragrance of a thousand flowers. Ahead of us, the rocky barriers all but meet, leaving a narrow rift where some giant hand seems to have torn them asunder. Through this narrow portal passes the stream, and even here we can catch the music of the falling waters. Drawing closer, we see a staircase clinging to the cliff, and entering the rift, we climb to an upper glen, wilder and more beautiful than its predecessor. Apparent danger is the sensation experienced by a visitor for the first time to this charming spot; but this soon gives way to admiration and delight, as every precaution has been taken to render a trip through the Glen entirely secure. The proper season for a visit is between the middle of May and the first of November. Ferns and mosses in almost endless varieties, and many of the former of immense proportions, abound here. Seneca Lake, lying close at hand, is a beautiful body of water, varying from two to six miles in width, and forty miles long. Elegant and commodious steamers, manned by polite and attentive officers, run uninterruptedly the whole length of the lake during the entire year, and all who can should, by all means, enjoy a ride on Seneca Lake, from Watkins' to Geneva.

The distance from New York to Watkins' Glen, via the Erie Railway, is two hundred and ninety-six miles; via New York Central and Hudson River Railroad, four hundred and fourteen miles; from Philadelphia, via Lehigh Valley Railroad, two hundred and eighty-seven miles; via Harrisburg, three hundred miles; from Baltimore, via Northern Central Railroad, two hundred and seventy-eight miles.

The visitor, on arrival at the railroad depot or steamboat landing at Watkins', inquires for the porter of the Glen Mountain House, who will take charge of his baggage and show him to the elegant coaches belonging to the house. Passing in one of these through the streets of the neat, pretty village, he comes to the foot of a hill, near the summit of which, nestling among hemlocks and other evergreens, about four hundred feet above the level of the lake, he will find that haven of rest and comfort, the Glen Mountain House.

This house is fitted up with all modern conveniences,—gas, hot and cold water baths, an abundance of pure water from the mountain springs; and, in addition to having the privileges of mountain air and scenery, guests of the house are at liberty to visit the Glen as often as may be desired during *their entire stay*, at the same price it would cost them *each time*, if stopping at any other house.

Besides Watkins' Glen, tourists may find in this vicinity other noted beautiful

THE GLEN MOUNTAIN HOUSE.

resorts,—Havana Glen, Glen Excelsior, Glenora, Hector, and Havana Falls, and many other charming spots where the lover of nature may find substantial enjoyment and profit. Havana Glen, about three miles distant from Watkins', may be reached by carriages, which can be obtained at the Glen Mountain House.

COOPERSTOWN, SHARON SPRINGS, RICHFIELD SPRINGS, TRENTON FALLS, ITHACA.—Nor, it may be added, can the tourist, after traversing the mountain regions of the Lehigh, find a more charming contrast than among the historic and beautiful scenes traversed by, or adjacent to, the line of the Albany and Susquehanna Railroad, extending from Albany to Binghamton, a distance of one hundred and forty-two miles. The traveler by the route we have sketched may, therefore, take this line, via the Erie Railway, from Waverly to Binghamton, going north, or, on his return from Lake Champlain, at Albany, going south. In either case it will carry him directly through the Otsego Lake region, rendered famous by Fenimore Cooper in his "Leatherstocking" series. Here he will find

COOPERSTOWN,

That author's former residence, high up in the mountains, in the midst of beautiful scenery, and provided with good hotels and refined society. Otsego Lake, on which the town is situated, is the source of the Susquehanna; is nine miles long, from one to two wide, and its waters abound in fish. At Cobleskill, forty-five miles from Albany, the tourist connects with Branch for

SHARON SPRINGS,

A curious feature of which place is the issuance of five different kinds of water from apertures near each other. They are white sulphur, blue sulphur, chalybeate, magnesia, and *aqua pura*. There are two first-class hotels at the Springs. Within a few miles drive, too, of Cooperstown, are

RICHFIELD SPRINGS,

A quiet but favorite resort, where a few weeks can be passed in enjoyment and comfort. It possesses the advantages of beautiful drives and rambles, and excellent boating, fishing, and bathing facilities. There is a good hotel on the Spring grounds.

TRENTON FALLS,

Too, are well worth visiting. Here the West Canada Creek, a branch of the Mohawk, has a fall of three hundred and twelve feet in two miles, by a series of six remarkably varied and beautiful cataracts. "In the long corridor of travel between New York and Niagara," once said N. P. Willis, "Trenton is a sort of alcove aside—a side-scene out of earshot of the crowd—a recess in a corridor whither you draw a friend by the button for the sake of chit-chat at ease."

ITHACA,

Too, abounds, in its suburbs, in varied and striking scenery, which we may reach by the Ithaca and Athens Railroad, from its junction, at Athens, with the Lehigh Valley Railroad. Situated at the head of Cayuga Lake, it has in its immediate vicinity no less than fifteen waterfalls, five of them one hundred feet, and one one hundred and sixty feet high. A visit to Taghanic Falls, a cataract exceeding Niagara in height by over fifty feet, will also amply recompense the tourist.

☞ For description of Routes and Rates of Fare, see pages 42–55.

COLORADO EXCURSIONS.

Go West through St. Louis.

DURING THE SUMMER SEASON

THE

MISSOURI PACIFIC and KANSAS PACIFIC THROUGH LINE

(Via ST. LOUIS and KANSAS CITY.)

Will sell Excursion Tickets from St. Louis to Denver and Return,

Good Ninety Days from date of sale, at Extremely Low Rates, thus affording every one an excellent opportunity to visit the Famous Resorts of Colorado among the Beautiful Parks of the Rocky Mountains.

To all who are seeking new homes in or are about to take a trip to **Missouri, Kansas, Colorado, New Mexico, Nebraska, Oregon, or California**, we recommend a Cheap, Safe, Quick, and Direct Route, by way of St. Louis, over the

MISSOURI PACIFIC THROUGH LINE.

It is equipped with FINE DAY COACHES, BUCK'S RECLINING-CHAIR CARS, PULLMAN'S PALACE SLEEPERS, the FAMOUS MILLER SAFETY PLATFORM, and the CELEBRATED WESTINGHOUSE AIR BRAKE, and runs its trains from St. Louis to principal points in the West **Without Change.** The Texas connection of this Road is now completed, and passengers are offered a first-class all-rail route from St. Louis to Texas, either over the **Missouri, Kansas & Texas R. R.**, via **Sedalia**, or over the **Atlantic & Pacific R. R.**, via **Vinita**.

For full information in regard to Colorado Excursions, or trips to any point in the Great West, address or call upon either of the following-named Agents of the line:—

J. F. THOMPSON,
157 Exchange St., Buffalo, N. Y.

S. H. THOMPSON,
Union Depot, Columbus, Ohio.

E. A. FORD, Gen'l Pass'r Agent,
25 South Fourth St., St. Louis, Mo.

☞ Questions will be cheerfully and promptly answered.

THE MANSION HOUSE,
MAUCH CHUNK, PA.

This House is now open for the reception of guests. Its location, in a region popularly termed the "SWITZERLAND OF AMERICA," and which combines with the most unsurpassed scenery the finest mountain air and the purest spring water to be found on the continent, commands for it an enviable reputation as a summer resort.

The famous Gravity Railroad, the oldest in the United States, and which passes over the mountains and through the coal fields of this section, affords the tens of thousands who are annually attracted to this resort the most delightful means of enjoying its world-renowned scenery.

Time from New York to Mauch Chunk only four hours, and from Philadelphia only three hours. Excursion Tickets, including a ride over the Gravity Railroad, $6.25 from New York, and $5 from Philadelphia.

E. T. BOOTH,
Mansion House, Mauch Chunk. **Proprietor.**

ELMIRA, N. Y.

S. H. WADSWORTH.

BUCK'S CELEBRATED RECLINING-CHAIR CAR,
RUN ON
ST. LOUIS, KANSAS CITY & NORTHERN SHORT LINE

This is the only line running Coaches built expressly for Buck's Reclining Chairs free of extra charge. These Coaches are elegantly carpeted and fitted with commodious dressing-rooms for ladies, gentlemen, and families traveling with children, WITHOUT ANY EXTRA CHARGE.

Pullman Sleeping Palaces on Night Trains.
SEE ADVERTISEMENT ANOTHER PAGE.

MEMPHREMAGOG HOUSE,
NEWPORT, VERMONT.

W. F. BOWMAN, Proprietor.

THIS wide-known and ever-popular Summer Resort is now opened for the season of 1874. It is situated in the northern part of Vermont, at the head of Lake Memphremagog, and five miles south of the line separating the Dominion of Canada from the United States. During the last spring this House has been entirely refurnished and refitted and placed in complete order in all its appointments, and it is now one of the largest and finest hotels in New England. It is four stories high, has a front of nearly 200 feet, and its broad piazzas command a charming view of lake and mountain scenery. There is nothing more gorgeous and beautiful than the sunset views obtained from the north piazzas, which overlook the lake. This House will easily accommodate 400 guests. It is supplied with water, gas, and steam, and is fitted up in every department with all the modern improvements and conveniences. In the basement, fronting on the park and lake, are billiard-rooms and bowling-alleys for both ladies and gentlemen. A fine livery stable, with the best of horses and carriages, is connected with this House; also, new and elegant row-boats.

The steamer Lady of the Lake, Capt. Geo. W. Fogg, commander, receives and lands passengers at the wharf, within 100 feet of this House. This splendid iron steamer makes two trips daily through the lake. The depots are only a few rods from this House. For trout-fishing there is no better place than Northern Vermont, and the small streams all about Newport and vicinity are filled with brook trout, which are caught in great abundance. Lake Memphremagog also abounds in trout, resembling the brook trout, and weighing from five to forty pounds,—and fishing for such trout is rare sport.

The walks and drives about Newport are unequaled for variety of scenery, and the view from Prospect Hill, south-west from this Hotel, is not excelled by any in New England. From it there is a good view of Joy Peak of the Green Mountain range, which is second in point of height of the mountains in Vermont, and is easily reached by carriage from Newport. Also, Lake Willoughby, twenty miles south, one of the most remarkable places on this continent, and which lies in the gorge of a high mountain, which, at some period of the earth's history, has been cut open. On each side of this lake are mountains rising almost perpendicularly nearly 2500 feet. On the east side there is just room enough between this lake and the frowning wall above for a carriage road. Newport may be most easily reached by the following routes:—

From New York, via Springfield and White River Junction. Distance, 369 miles.
From Boston, via Concord and White River Junction, or via Concord, Plymouth, and Wells River.
From the White Mountains, via Wells River.
From Saratoga Springs, via Burlington, St. Alban's, and Richford.
From Montreal, via South-Eastern Railway.
From Quebec, via Grand Trunk and Connecticut & Passumpsic Rivers and Massawippi Valley Railways.

No summer resort in New England is easier of access or has better railroad facilities and accommodations than Newport. The Connecticut & Passumpsic Rivers Railroad and the South-Eastern Railway run Pullman Palace Cars on all trains.

W. S. PURVIANCE,
Photographer and Publisher
OF
NOTED AMERICAN SCENERY,
For the Stereoscope and Graphoscope,

1929 NORTH TWELFTH STREET, PHILADELPHIA.

TOURISTS

Will find at "PURVIANCE'S" the best and most complete sets of Stereoscopic Views of the various

POPULAR SUMMER RESORTS,
EMBRACING THE SCENERY OF

WATKINS' GLEN,	PASSAIC FALLS,
HAVANA GLEN,	ERIE RAILWAY,
GLEN ONOKO,	PENNSYLVANIA R. R.,
AU SABLE CHASM,	LEHIGH VALLEY R. R.,
DELAWARE WATER GAP,	SWITCHBACK R. R.,
NIAGARA FALLS,	PHILADELPHIA AND
GENESEE FALLS,	VICINITY, &c., &c.

New Subjects are being Constantly Added.

Full sets of these Views are kept on sale during the season at

Watkins' Glen, Mauch Chunk, Au Sable Chasm, and other Watering-Places

And can be had of dealers in every city in the country.

GREAT DOUBLE-TRACK ROUTE!
LAKE SHORE
AND
MICHIGAN SOUTHERN RAILWAY.

This Line, in combination with other roads, forms an ALL-RAIL Through Route, without ferry transfers, besides enjoying the most favorable geographical position on the most natural line of communication between the great business centres East, West, South-west, and across the continent. It makes more direct connections through Union Depots than any other Western Railway. It is the only line connecting with the New York Central and Erie Railways which runs ALL CARS of

EXPRESS TRAINS THROUGH TO CHICAGO

avoiding ferry transfers, and affording equal advantages to all classes of passengers in avoiding changes.

ALL MODERN IMPROVEMENTS ON THIS LINE.

THIS RAILWAY CONNECTS
WITH

ALL TRAINS FROM THE EAST

4 Express Trains Daily
THROUGH TO
CHICAGO.

2 SUNDAY TRAINS
FOR
Cleveland, Toledo, & Chicago.

FRONT VIEW OF L. S. & M. S. R'Y DEPOT, CHICAGO.

Passengers for Chicago arrive in the magnificent New Depot in the heart of the city.

Through Tickets by this Favorite Route for sale at all principal offices.

J. A. BURCH,   CHAS. PAINE,
General Eastern Passenger Agent.   *General Superintendent.*

THE OHIO & MISSISSIPPI RAILWAY.

THE GREAT THROUGH PASSENGER ROUTE BETWEEN THE EAST AND WEST.

SHORT LINE

CINCINNATI TO
EVANSVILLE,
CAIRO,
ST. LOUIS,
LITTLE ROCK
HOT SP'NGS,
KANSAS CITY
DENNISON,
DENVER,
OMAHA,
And all points IN
COLORADO
AND
CALIFORNIA.

DIRECT AND Best Route

CINCINNATI TO
LOUISVILLE,
NASHVILLE,
CHATTANOOGA
ATLANTA,
MONTGOMERY,
MOBILE,
NEW ORLEANS
GALVESTON,
SHREVEPORT
MEMPHIS,
And all points IN THE
SOUTH AND South-east.

Connections are perfect and reliable, and trains are run to make this Line a direct and desirable route between the

EAST, WEST, AND SOUTH

FOR ALL CLASSES OF PASSENGERS.

View of the great Steel Bridge across the Mississippi River at St. Louis.

THE WESTERN TERMINUS OF THE OHIO & MISSISSIPPI RAILWAY.

The entire trains of this Company run through

CINCINNATI TO ST. LOUIS

WITHOUT CHANGE.

Pullman Palace Sleeping Cars on Night Trains.

THROUGH TICKETS ARE ON SALE BY THIS POPULAR LINE AT ALL PRINCIPAL TICKET OFFICES IN THE EAST.

SEASON OF 1874.

COMBINATION EXCURSION TARIFF

OF THE

ERIE RAILWAY

FROM PHILADELPHIA,

IN CONNECTION WITH THE

LEHIGH VALLEY AND NORTH PENNSYLVANIA RAILROADS.

PRINCIPAL OFFICE OF THE COMPANY IN PHILADELPHIA,

732 Chestnut Street, S. E. corner Eighth Street.

EXCURSION TICKETS ARE GOOD DURING THE PLEASURE SEASON, (JUNE 1ST TO NOVEMBER 1ST,) UNLESS OTHERWISE LIMITED, AND HAVE ALL THE PRIVILEGES OF FIRST CLASS TICKETS.

TICKETS PASSING OVER LAKE ONTARIO AND RIVER ST. LAWRENCE, BETWEEN TORONTO AND MONTREAL, INCLUDE MEALS; BUT BETWEEN MONTREAL AND QUEBEC THEY ARE FOR PASSAGE ONLY. BERTHS ARE INCLUDED ON FALL RIVER LINE STEAMERS BETWEEN NEWPORT AND NEW YORK.

NIAGARA FALLS EXCURSIONS.

EXCURSION P 1.—*Philadelphia to Niagara Falls and return to Philadelphia;* via North Penna. R. R. to Bethlehem; Lehigh Valley R. R. to Waverly, and Erie Railway to Niagara Falls; *returning* by same route as in going..$17.50.

EXCURSION P 5.—*Philadelphia to Niagara Falls and return to Philadelphia;* via North Penna. R. R. to Bethlehem; Lehigh Valley R. R. to Waverly; Erie Railway to Elmira; Can. Div. Nor. Cent. R. W. to Canandaigua, and New York Central R. R. to Niagara Falls; *returning* via Erie Railway to Waverly; Lehigh Valley R. R. to Bethlehem, and North Penna. R. R. to Philadelphia...$19.50.

EXCURSION P 9.—*Philadelphia to Niagara Falls and return to Philadelphia;* via North Penna. R. R. to Bethlehem; Lehigh Valley R. R. to Athens; Southern Central R. R. to Auburn, and New York Central R. R. to Niagara Falls; *returning* via Erie Railway to Waverly; Lehigh Valley R. R. to Bethlehem, and North Penna R. R. to Philadelphia............$19.50.

EXCURSION P 10.—*Philadelphia to Niagara Falls and return to Philadelphia;* via North Penna. R. R. to Bethlehem; Lehigh Valley R. R. to Waverly Junction; Ithaca & Athens R. R. to Ithaca; Cayuga Lake Steamers to Cayuga, and New York Central R. R. to Niagara Falls; *returning* via Erie Railway to Waverly; Lehigh Valley R. R. to Bethlehem, and North Penna. R. R. to Philadelphia...$19.50.

EXCURSION P 11.—*Philadelphia to Niagara Falls and return to Philadelphia;* via North Penna. R. R. to Bethlehem; Lehigh Valley R. R. to Waverly; Erie Railway to Elmira; Can. Div. Nor. Cent. R. W. to Watkins'; Seneca Lake Steamers to Geneva, and New York Central R. R. to Niagara Falls; *returning* via Erie Railway to Waverly; Lehigh Valley R. R. to Bethlehem, and North Penna. R. R. to Philadelphia............................$18.00.

EXCURSION P 15.—*Philadelphia to Niagara Falls and return to Philadelphia;* via North Penna. R. R. to Bethlehem; Lehigh Valley R. R. to Waverly, and Erie Railway to Niagara Falls; *returning* via New York Central R. R. to Canandaigua; Can. Div. Nor. Cent. R. W. to Elmira; Erie Railway to Waverly; Lehigh Valley R. R. to Bethlehem, and North Penna. R. R. to Philadelphia..$19.50.

EXCURSION P 19.—*Philadelphia to Niagara Falls and return to Philadelphia;* via North Penna. R. R. to Bethlehem; Lehigh Valley R. R. to Waverly, and Erie Railway to Niagara Falls; *returning* via New York Central R. R. to Geneva; Seneca Lake Steamers to Watkins'; Can. Div. Nor. Cent. R. W. to Elmira; Erie Railway to Waverly; Lehigh Valley R. R. to Bethlehem, and North Penna. R. R. to Philadelphia.............................$18.00.

EXCURSION P 23.—*Philadelphia to Niagara Falls and return to Philadelphia;* via North Penna. R. R. to Bethlehem; Lehigh Valley R. R. to Waverly, and Erie Railway to Niagara Falls; *returning* via New York Central R. R. to Auburn; Southern Central R. R. to Athens; Lehigh Valley R. R. to Bethlehem, and North Penna. R. R. to Philadelphia..........$19.50.

EXCURSION P 24.—*Philadelphia to Niagara Falls and return to Philadelphia;* via North Penna. R. R. to Bethlehem; Lehigh Valley R. R. to Waverly, and Erie Railway to Niagara Falls; *returning* via New York Central R. R. to Cayuga; Cayuga Lake Steamers to Ithaca; Ithaca & Athens R. R. to Waverly Junction; Lehigh Valley R. R. to Bethlehem, and North Penna. R. R. to Philadelphia..$19.50.

EXCURSION P 25.—*Philadelphia to Niagara Falls and return to Philadelphia;* via North Penna. R. R. to Bethlehem; Lehigh Valley R. R. to Waverly, and Erie Railway to Niagara Falls; *returning* via Erie Railway to Elmira; Elmira & Williamsport R. R. to Williamsport; Phila. & Erie R. R. to Sunbury; Nor. Cent. R. W. to Harrisburg, and Penna. R. R. to Philadelphia..$19.50.

EXCURSION P 26.—*Philadelphia to Niagara Falls and return to Philadelphia;* via North Penna. R. R. to Bethlehem; Lehigh Valley R. R. to Waverly, and Erie Railway to Niagara Falls; *returning* via Erie Railway to Elmira; Elmira & Williamsport R. R. to Williamsport, and Phila. & Reading R. R. to Philadelphia..$19.50.

EXCURSION P 27.—*Philadelphia to Niagara Falls and return to Philadelphia;* via North Penna. R. R. to Bethlehem; Lehigh Valley R. R. to Waverly, and Erie Railway to Niagara Falls; *returning* via Erie Railway to Binghamton; D., L. & W. R. R. to Manunka Chunk, and Bel. Div. Penna. R. R. to Philadelphia..$19.50.

EXCURSION P 29.—*Philadelphia to Niagara Falls and return to Philadelphia;* via Phila. & Reading R. R. to Williamsport; Elmira & Williamsport R. R. to Elmira, and Erie Railway to Niagara Falls; *returning* via Erie Railway to Waverly; Lehigh Valley R. R. to Bethlehem, and North Penna. R. R. to Philadelphia............................!............$19.50.

EXCURSION P 37.—*Philadelphia to Niagara Falls and return to Philadelphia;* via North Penna. R. R. to Bethlehem; Lehigh Valley R. R. to Waverly, and Erie Railway to Niagara Falls; *returning* via Erie Railway to Buffalo; Buffalo, New York & Philadelphia R. R. to Emporium; Phila. & Erie R. R. to Sunbury; Nor. Cent. R. W. to Harrisburg, and Penna. R. R. to Philadelphia...$19.50.

EXCURSION P 44.—*Philadelphia to Niagara Falls and return to Philadelphia;* via North Penna. R. R. to Bethlehem; Lehigh Valley R. R. to Waverly, and Erie Railway to Niagara Falls; *returning* via Erie Railway to New York, and N. Y. Div. Penna. R. R. to Philadelphia...$20.75.

EXCURSION P 48.—*Philadelphia to Niagara Falls and return to Philadelphia;* via North Penna. R. R. to Bethlehem; Lehigh Valley R. R. to Waverly, and Erie Railway to Niagara Falls; *returning* via New York Central R. R. to Albany; Hudson River Steamers to New York, and N. Y. Div. Penna. R. R. to Philadelphia..................$20.75.

EXCURSION P 52.—*Philadelphia to Niagara Falls and return to Philadelphia;* via North Penna. R. R. to Bethlehem; Lehigh Valley R. R. to Waverly, and Erie Railway to Niagara Falls; *returning* via New York Central R. R. to New York, and N. Y. Div. Penna. R. R. to Philadelphia..................$20.75.

EXCURSION P 53.—*Philadelphia to Niagara Falls and return to Philadelphia;* via North Penna. R. R. to Bethlehem; Lehigh Valley R. R. to Waverly, and Erie Railway to Niagara Falls; *returning* via Erie Railway to Binghamton; Albany & Sus. R. R. to Albany; Hudson River Steamers to New York, and N. Y. Div. Penna. R. R. to Philadelphia..................$20.75.

EXCURSION P 56.—*Philadelphia to Niagara Falls and return to Philadelphia;* via North Penna. R. R. to Bethlehem; Lehigh Valley R. R. to Waverly; Erie Railway to Elmira; Can. Div. Nor. Cent. R. W. to Watkins'; Seneca Lake Steamers to Geneva, and New York Central R. R. to Niagara Falls; *returning* via Erie Railway to Binghamton; Albany & Sus. R. R. to Albany; Hudson River Steamers to New York, and N. Y. Div. Penna. R. R. to Philadelphia..................$20.75.

EXCURSION P 57.—*Philadelphia to Niagara Falls and return to Philadelphia;* via North Penna. R. R. to Bethlehem; Lehigh Valley R. R. to Waverly, and Erie Railway to Niagara Falls; *returning* via New York Central R. R. to Geneva; Seneca Lake Steamers to Watkins'; Can. Div. Nor. Cent. R. W. to Elmira; Erie Railway to Binghamton; Albany & Sus. R. R. to Albany; Hudson River Steamers to New York, and N. Y. Div. Penna. R. R. to Philadelphia..................$23.65.

EXCURSION P 58.—*Philadelphia to Niagara Falls and return to Philadelphia;* via North Penna. R. R. to Bethlehem; Lehigh Valley R. R. to Waverly, and Erie Railway to Niagara Falls; *returning* via New York Central R. R. to Canandaigua; Can. Div. Nor. Cent. R. W. to Elmira; Erie Railway to Binghamton; Albany & Sus. R. R. to Albany; Hudson River Steamers to New York, and N. Y. Div. Penna. R. R. to Philadelphia..................$23.65.

EXCURSION P 59.—*Philadelphia to Niagara Falls and return to Philadelphia;* via North Penna. R. R. to Bethlehem; Lehigh Valley R. R. to Waverly; Erie Railway to Elmira; Can. Div. Nor. Cent. R. W. to Canandaigua, and New York Central R. R. to Niagara Falls; *returning* via Erie Railway to Binghamton; Albany & Sus. R. R. to Albany; Hudson River Steamers to New York, and N. Y. Div. Penna. R. R. to Philadelphia..................$20.75.

EXCURSION P 60.—*Philadelphia to Niagara Falls and return to Philadelphia;* via North Penna. R. R. to Bethlehem; Lehigh Valley R. R. to Waverly Junction; Ithaca & Athens R. R. to Ithaca; Cayuga Lake Steamers to Cayuga, and New York Central R. R. to Niagara Falls; *returning* via Erie Railway to Binghamton; Albany & Sus. R. R. to Albany; Hudson River Steamers to New York, and N. Y. Div. Penna. R. R. to Philadelphia...$20.75.

EXCURSION P 61.—*Philadelphia to Niagara Falls and return to Philadelphia;* via North Penna. R. R. to Bethlehem; Lehigh Valley R. R. to Waverly, and Erie Railway to Niagara Falls; *returning* via New York Central R. R. to Utica; D., L. & W. R. R. to Richfield Springs; Otsego Lake Steamers to Cooperstown; C. & S. Valley R. R. to Junction; Albany & Sus. R. R. to Albany; Hudson River Steamers to New York, and N. Y. Div. Penna. R. R. to Philadelphia..................$23.25.

EXCURSION P 62.—*Philadelphia to Niagara Falls and return to Philadelphia;* via North Penna. R. R. to Bethlehem; Lehigh Valley R. R. to Waverly, and Erie Railway to Niagara Falls; *returning* via New York Central R. R. to Utica; D., L. & W. R. R. to Richfield Springs; Otsego Lake Steamers to Cooperstown; C. & S. Valley R. R. to Junction; Albany & Sus. R. R. to Binghamton; D., L. & W. R. R. to Manunka Chunk, and Bel. Div. Penna. R. R. to Philadelphia..................$23.10.

EXCURSION P 63.—*Philadelphia to Niagara Falls and return to Philadelphia;* via North Penna. R. R. to Bethlehem; Lehigh Valley R. R. to Waverly, and Erie Railway to Niagara Falls; *returning* via New York Central R. R. to Cayuga; Cayuga Lake Steamers to Ithaca; D., L. & W. R. R. to Owego; Erie Railway to Binghamton; D., L. & W. R. R. to Manunka Chunk, and Bel. Div. Penna. R. R. to Philadelphia..................$20.25.

EXCURSION P 64.—*Philadelphia to Niagara Falls and return to Philadelphia;* via North Penna. R. R. to Bethlehem; Lehigh Valley R. R. to Waverly, and Erie Railway to Niagara Falls; *returning* via Erie Railway to Binghamton; Albany & Sus. R. R. to Sharon Springs, and thence to Albany; Hudson River Steamers to New York, and N. Y. Div. Penna. R. R. to Philadelphia..$21.30.

EXCURSION P 65.—*Philadelphia to Niagara Falls and return to Philadelphia;* via North Penna. R. R. to Bethlehem; Lehigh Valley R. R. to Waverly, and Erie Railway to Niagara Falls; *returning* via Erie Railway to Binghamton; Albany & Sus. R. R. to Albany; Rens. & Saratoga R. R. to Saratoga and back to Albany; Hudson River Steamers to New York and N. Y. Div. Penna. R. R. to Philadelphia..$23.15.

EXCURSION P 66.—*Philadelphia to Niagara Falls and return to Philadelphia;* via North Penna. R. R. to Bethlehem; Lehigh Valley R. R. to Waverly, and Erie Railway to Niagara Falls; *returning* via New York Central R. R. to Schenectady; Rens. & Saratoga R. R. to Saratoga and thence to Albany; Hudson River Steamers to New York, and N. Y. Div. Penna. R. R. to Philadelphia...$22.55.

EXCURSION P 67.—*Philadelphia to Niagara Falls and return to Philadelphia;* via North Penna. R. R. to Bethlehem; Lehigh Valley R. R. to Waverly, and Erie Railway to Niagara Falls; *returning* via New York Central R. R. to Utica; D., L. & W. R. R. to Richfield Springs; Otsego Lake Steamers to Cooperstown; C. & S. Valley R. R. to Junction; Albany & Sus. R. R. to Albany; Rens. & Saratoga R. R. to Saratoga and back to Albany; Hudson River Steamers to New York, and N. Y. Div. Penna. R. R. to Philadelphia.....................$25.65.

EXCURSION P 68.—*Philadelphia to Niagara Falls and return to Philadelphia;* via North Penna. R. R. to Bethlehem; Lehigh Valley R. R. to Waverly, and Erie Railway to Niagara Falls; *returning* via New York Central R. R. to Utica; D., L. & W. R. R. to Richfield Springs; Otsego Lake Steamers to Cooperstown; C. & S. Valley R. R. to Junction; Albany & Sus. R. R. to Binghamton; Erie Railway to New York, and N. Y. Div. Penna. R. R. to Philadelphia ....$25.40.

EXCURSION P 69.—*Philadelphia to Niagara Falls and return to Philadelphia;* via North Penna. R. R. to Bethlehem; Lehigh Valley R. R. to Waverly, and Erie Railway to Niagara Falls; *returning* via New York Central R. R. to Utica; Utica & Black River R. R. to Trenton Falls and back to Utica; D., L. & W. R. R. to Richfield Springs; Otsego Lake Steamers to Cooperstown; C. & S. Valley R. R. to Junction; Albany & Sus. R. R. to Albany; Hudson River Steamers to New York, and N. Y. Div. Penna. R. R. to Philadelphia...........$24.25.

EXCURSION P 70.—*Philadelphia to Niagara Falls and return to Philadelphia;* via North Penna. R. R. to Bethlehem; Lehigh Valley R. R. to Waverly, and Erie Railway to Niagara Falls; *returning* via New York Central R. R. to Utica; Utica & Black River R. R. to Trenton Falls and back to Utica; New York Central R. R. to Schenectady; Rens. & Saratoga R. R. to Saratoga and back to Albany; Hudson River Steamers to New York, and N. Y. Div. Penna. R. R. to Philadelphia..$23.55.

EXCURSION P 71.—*Philadelphia to Niagara Falls and return to Philadelphia;* via North Penna. R. R. to Bethlehem; Lehigh Valley R. R. to Waverly, and Erie Railway to Niagara Falls; *returning* via New York Central R. R. to Utica; Utica & Black River R. R. to Trenton Falls and back to Utica; D., L. & W. R. R. to Binghamton and thence to Manunka Chunk, and Bel. Div. Penna. R. R. to Philadelphia...............................$21.90.

EXCURSION P 72.—*Philadelphia to Niagara Falls and return to Philadelphia;* via North Penna. R. R. to Bethlehem; Lehigh Valley R. R. to Waverly; Erie Railway to Elmira; Can. Div. Nor. Cent. R. W. to Watkins' and back to Elmira, and Erie Railway to Niagara Falls; *returning* via Erie Railway to Waverly; Lehigh Valley R. R. to Bethlehem, and North Penna. R. R. to Philadelphia...$17.50.

EXCURSION P 75.—*Philadelphia to Niagara Falls and return to Philadelphia;* via North Penna. R. R. to Bethlehem; Lehigh Valley R. R. to Waverly, and Erie Railway to Niagara Falls; *returning* via New York Central R. R. to Canandaigua; Can. Div. Nor. Cent. R. W. to Elmira; Elmira & Williamsport R. R. to Williamsport; Phila. & Erie R. R. to Sunbury; Nor. Cent. R. W. to Harrisburg, and Penna. R. R. to Philadelphia....................$19.50.

EXCURSION P 76.—*Philadelphia to Niagara Falls and return to Philadelphia;* via North Penna. R. R. to Bethlehem; Lehigh Valley R. R. to Waverly, and Erie Railway to Niagara Falls; *returning* via New York Central R. R. to Canandaigua; Can. Div. Nor. Cent. R. W. to Elmira; Elmira & Williamsport R. R. to Williamsport, and Phila. & Reading R. R. to Philadelphia..$19.50.

EXCURSION P 77.—*Philadelphia to Niagara Falls and return to Philadelphia;* via North Penna. R. R. to Bethlehem; Lehigh Valley R. R. to Waverly, and Erie Railway to Niagara Falls; *returning* via New York Central R. R. to Geneva; Seneca Lake Steamers to Watkins'; Can. Div. Nor. Cen. R. W. to Elmira; Elmira & Williamsport R. R. to Williamsport; Phila. & Erie R. R. to Sunbury; Nor. Cent. R. W. to Harrisburg, and Penna. R. R. to Philadelphia...$19.50.

EXCURSION P 78.—*Philadelphia to Niagara Falls and return to Philadelphia;* via North Penna. R. R. to Bethlehem; Lehigh Valley R. R. to Waverly, and Erie Railway to Niagara Falls; *returning* via New York Central R. R. to Geneva; Seneca Lake Steamers to Watkins'; Can. Div. Nor. Cent. R. W. to Elmira; Elmira & Williamsport R. W. to Williamsport, and Phila. & Reading R. R. to Philadelphia...$19.50.

EXCURSION P 80.—*Philadelphia to Niagara Falls and return to Philadelphia;* via Phila. & Reading R. R to Williamsport; Elmira & Williamsport R. R. to Elmira; Can. Div. Nor. Cent. R. W. to Watkins'; Seneca Lake Steamers to Geneva, and New York Central R. R. to Niagara Falls; *returning* via Erie Railway to Waverly; Lehigh Valley R. R. to Bethlehem and North Penna. R. R. to Philadelphia...$19.50.

EXCURSION P 119.—*Philadelphia to Niagara Falls and return to Philadelphia;* via North Penna. R. R. to Bethlehem; Lehigh Valley R. R. to Waverly, and Erie Railway to Niagara Falls; *returning* via Erie Railway to Bath; Stage to Hammondsport; Lake Keuka Steamer to Penn Yan; Nor. Cent. R. W. to Elmira; Erie Railway to Waverly; Lehigh Valley R. R. to Bethlehem, and North Penna. R. R. to Philadelphia......................$20.80.

EXCURSION P 129.—*Philadelphia to Niagara Falls and return to Philadelphia;* via North Penna. R. R. to Bethlehem; Lehigh Valley R. R. to Waverly; Erie Railway to Elmira; Nor. Cent. R. W. to Watkins'; Seneca Lake Steamers to Geneva, and New York Central R. R. to Niagara Falls; *returning* via Erie Railway to New York, and Penna. R. R. to Philadelphia...$20.75.

COOPERSTOWN EXCURSIONS.

EXCURSION P 81.—*Philadelphia to Cooperstown and return to Philadelphia;* via North Penna. R. R. to Bethlehem; Lehigh Valley R. R. to Waverly; Erie Railway to Binghamton; Albany & Sus. R. R. to Junction, and C. & S. Valley R. R. to Cooperstown; *returning* via C. & S. Valley R. R. to Junction; Albany & Sus. R. R. to Binghamton; D., L. & W. R. R. to Manunka Chunk, and Bel. Div. Penna. R. R. to Philadelphia....................$15.35.

EXCURSION P 82.—*Philadelphia to Cooperstown and return to Philadelphia;* via North Penna. R. R. to Bethlehem; Lehigh Valley R. R. to Waverly; Erie Railway to Binghamton; Albany & Sus. R. R. to Junction, and C. & S. Valley R. R. to Cooperstown; *returning* via C. & S. Valley R. R. to Junction; Albany & Sus. R. R. to Albany; Hudson River Steamers to New York, and N. Y. Div. Penna. R. R. to Philadelphia........................$15.70.

RICHFIELD SPRINGS EXCURSIONS.

EXCURSION P 83.—*Philadelphia to Richfield Springs and return to Philadelphia;* via North Penna. R. R. to Bethlehem; Lehigh Valley R. R. to Waverly; Erie Railway to Binghamton; Albany & Sus. R. R. to Junction; C. & S. Valley R. R. to Cooperstown, and Otsego Lake Steamers to Richfield Springs; *returning* via D., L. & W. R. R. to Utica; New York Central R. R. to Albany; Hudson River Steamers to New York, and N. Y. Div. Penna. R. R. to Philadelphia..$17.25.

EXCURSION P 84.—*Philadelphia to Richfield Springs and return to Philadelphia;* via North Penna. R. R. to Bethlehem; Lehigh Valley R. R. to Waverly; Erie Railway to Binghamton; Albany & Sus. R. R. to Junction; C. & S. Valley R. R. to Cooperstown, and Otsego Lake Steamers to Richfield Springs; *returning* via D. L. & W. R. R. to Utica; New York Central R. R. to Geneva; Seneca Lake Steamers to Watkins'; Can. Div. Nor. Cent. R. W. to Elmira; Elmira & Williamsport R. R. to Williamsport; Phila. & Erie R. R. to Sunbury; Nor. Cent. R. W. to Harrisburg, and Penna. R. R. to Philadelphia...$21.15.

SHARON SPRINGS EXCURSIONS.

EXCURSION P 85.—*Philadelphia to Sharon Springs and return to Philadelphia;* via North Penna. R. R. to Bethlehem; Lehigh Valley R. R. to Waverly; Erie Railway to Binghamton, and Albany & Sus. R. R. to Sharon Springs; *returning* via Otsego Lake Steamers to Cooperstown; C. & S. Valley R. R. to Junction; Albany & Sus. R. R. to Binghamton; D., L. & W. R. R. to Manunka Chunk, and Bel. Div. Penna. R. R. to Philadelphia..........$16.90.

EXCURSION P 86.—*Philadelphia to Sharon Springs and return to Philadelphia;* via North Penna. R. R. to Bethlehem; Lehigh Valley R. R. to Waverly; Erie Railway to Binghamton, and Albany & Sus. R. R. to Sharon Springs; *returning* via Albany & Sus. R. R. to Albany; Hudson River Steamers to New York, and N. Y. Div. Penna. R. R. to Philadelphia..$14.65.

SARATOGA EXCURSIONS.

EXCURSION P 87.—*Philadelphia to Saratoga Springs and return to Philadelphia;* via North Penna. R. R. to Bethlehem; Lehigh Valley R. R. to Waverly; Erie Railway to Binghamton; Albany & Sus. R. R. to Albany, and Rens. & Saratoga R. R. to Saratoga; *returning* via Rens. & Saratoga R. R. to Albany; Hudson River Steamers to New York, and N. Y. Div. Penna. R. R. to Philadelphia...$16.50.

EXCURSION P 88.—*Philadelphia to Saratoga Springs and return to Philadelphia;* via North Penna. R. R. to Bethlehem; Lehigh Valley R. R. to Waverly; Erie Railway to Binghamton; Albany & Sus. R. R. to Junction; C. & S. Valley R. R. to Cooperstown; Otsego Lake Steamers to Richfield Springs; D., L. & W. R. R. to Utica; New York Central R. R. to Schenectady, and Rens. & Saratoga R. R. to Saratoga Springs; *returning* via Rens. & Saratoga R. R. to Albany; Hudson River Steamers to New York, and N. Y. Div. Penna. R. R. to Philadelphia...$18.95.

CLIFTON SPRINGS AND ITHACA EXCURSIONS.

EXCURSION P 89.—*Philadelphia to Clifton Springs and return to Philadelphia;* via North Penna. R. R. to Bethlehem; Lehigh Valley R. R. to Waverly; Erie Railway to Elmira; Can. Div. Nor. Cent. R. W. to Watkins'; Seneca Lake Steamers to Geneva, and New York Central R. R. to Clifton Springs; *returning* via New York Central R. R. to Canandaigua; Can. Div. Nor. Cent. R. W. to Elmira; Erie Railway to Waverly; Lehigh Valley R. R. to Bethlehem, and North Penna. R. R. to Philadelphia..................................$15.40.

EXCURSION P 92.—*Philadelphia to Ithaca and return to Philadelphia;* via North Penna. R. R. to Bethlehem; Lehigh Valley R. R. to Waverly Junction, and Ithaca & Athens R. R. to Ithaca; *returning* via D., L. & W. R. R. to Owego; Erie Railway to Binghamton; D., L. & W. R. R. to Manunka Chunk, and Bel. Div. Penna R. R. to Philadelphia..............$12.65.

GENEVA EXCURSIONS.

EXCURSION P 132.—*Philadelphia to Geneva and return to Philadelphia;* via North Penna. R. R. to Bethlehem; Lehigh Valley R. R. to Waverly; Erie Railway to Elmira; Northern Central R. R. to Watkins', and Seneca Lake Steamers to Geneva; *returning* via Geneva, Ithaca & Athens R. R. to Ithaca; D., L. & W. R. R. to Owego; Erie Railway to Binghamton; D., L. & W. R. R. to Manunka Chunk, and Penna. R. R. to Philadelphia...$14.65.

EXCURSION P 133.—*Philadelphia to Geneva and return to Philadelphia;* via North Penna. R. R. to Bethlehem; Lehigh Valley R. R. to Waverly; Erie Railway to Elmira; Northern Central R. R. to Watkins', and Seneca Lake Steamers to Geneva; *returning* by same route as in going..$13.50.

EXCURSION P 93.—*Philadelphia to Geneva and return to Philadelphia;* via North Penna. R. R. to Bethlehem; Lehigh Valley R. R. to Waverly; Erie Railway to Elmira; Can. Div. Nor. Cent. R. W. to Watkins', and Seneca Lake Steamers to Geneva; *returning* via New York Central R. R. to Cayuga; Cayuga Lake Steamers to Ithaca; D., L. & W. R. R. to Owego; Erie Railway to Binghamton; D, L. & W. R. R. to Manunka Chunk, and Bel. Div. Penna. R. R. to Philadelphia..$15.15.

TRENTON FALLS EXCURSIONS.

EXCURSION P 90.—*Philadelphia to Trenton Falls and return to Philadelphia;* via North Penna. R. R. to Bethlehem; Lehigh Valley R. R. to Waverly; Erie Railway to Binghamton; D., L. & W. R. R. to Utica, and Utica & Black River R. R. to Trenton Falls; *returning* via Utica & Black River R. R. to Utica; D., L. & W. R. R. to Richfield Springs; Otsego Lake Steamers to Cooperstown; C. & S. Valley R. R. to Junction; Albany & Sus. R. R. to Binghamton; D., L. & W. R. R. to Manunka Chunk, and Bel. Div. Penna. R. R. to Philadelphia...$18.25.

EXCURSION P 91.—*Philadelphia to Trenton Falls and return to Philadelphia;* via North Penna. R. R. to Bethlehem; Lehigh Valley R. R. to Waverly; Erie Railway to Binghamton; Albany & Sus. R. R. to Junction; C. & S. Valley R. R. to Cooperstown; Otsego Lake Steamers to Richfield Springs; D., L. & W. R. R. to Utica, and Utica & Black River R. R. to Trenton Falls; *returning* via Utica & Black River R. R. to Utica; New York Central R. R. to Albany; Hudson River Steamers to New York, and N. Y. Div. Penna. R. R. to Philadelphia...$18.25.

WATKINS' GLEN EXCURSIONS.

EXCURSION P 94.—*Philadelphia to Watkins' Glen and return to Philadelphia;* via North Penna. R. R. to Bethlehem; Lehigh Valley R. R. to Waverly; Erie Railway to Elmira, and Can. Div. Nor. Cent. R. W. to Watkins'; *returning* by same route as in going................$12.00.

EXCURSION P 95.—*Philadelphia to Watkins' Glen and return to Philadelphia;* via North Penna. R. R. to Bethlehem; Lehigh Valley R. R. to Waverly; Erie Railway to Elmira, and Can. Div. Nor. Cent. R. W. to Watkins'; *returning* via Can. Div. Nor. Cent. R. W. to Elmira; Erie Railway to Binghamton; Albany & Sus. R. R. to Albany; Hudson River Steamers to New York, and N. Y. Div. Penna. R. R. to Philadelphia.......................... ....$16.50.

EXCURSION P 97.—*Philadelphia to Watkins' Glen and return to Philadelphia;* via North Penna. R. R. to Bethlehem; Lehigh Valley R. R. to Waverly; Erie Railway to Elmira, and Can. Div. Nor. Cent. R. W. to Watkins'; *returning* via Can. Div. Nor. Cent. R. W. to Elmira; Erie Railway to Binghamton; D., L. & W. R. R. to Manunka Chunk, and Bel. Div. Penna. R. R. to Philadelphia..$13.65.

EXCURSION P 98.—*Philadelphia to Watkins' Glen and return to Philadelphia;* via North Penna. R. R. to Bethlehem; Lehigh Valley R. R. to Waverly; Erie Railway to Elmira, and Can. Div. Nor. Cent. R. W. to Watkins'; *returning* via Seneca Lake Steamers to Geneva; New York Central R. R. to Utica; D., L. & W. R. R. to Richfield Springs; Otsego Lake Steamers to Cooperstown; C. & S. Valley R. R. to Junction; Albany & Sus. R. R. to Binghamton; Erie Railway to Waverly; Lehigh Valley R. R. to Bethlehem, and North Penna. R. R. to Philadelphia...:..$19.65.

EXCURSION P 121.—*Philadelphia to Watkins' Glen and return to Philadelphia;* via North Penna. R. R. to Bethlehem; Lehigh Valley R. R. to Waverly; Erie Railway to Elmira, and Nor. Cent. R. W. to Watkins'; *returning* via Nor. Cent. R. W. to Elmira; Erie Railway to New York, and N. Y. Div. Penna. R. R. to Philadelphia.................................$16.50.

HAVANA GLEN EXCURSION.

EXCURSION P 120.—*Philadelphia to Havana (Montour Springs and Glens);* via North Penna. R. R. to Bethlehem; Lehigh Valley R. R. to Waverly; Erie Railway to Elmira, and Nor. Cent. R. W. to Havana; *returning* by same route as in going...........................$11.80.

MONTREAL EXCURSIONS.

EXCURSION P 99.—*Philadelphia to Montreal and return to Philadelphia;* via North Penna R. R. to Bethlehem; Lehigh Valley R. R. to Waverly; Erie Railway to Niagara Falls; New York Central R. R. to Lewiston; steamer to Toronto, and Grand Trunk R. W. or Royal Mail Line Steamers to Montreal; *returning* via Grand Trunk R. W. to Rouse's Point; Lake Champlain Steamers to Whitehall; Rens. & Saratoga R. R. to Saratoga and Albany; Hudson River Steamers to New York, and N. Y. Div. Penna. R. R. to Philadelphia.
$36.25.

EXCURSION P 100.—*Philadelphia to Montreal and return to Philadelphia;* via North Penna. R. R. to Bethlehem; Lehigh Valley R. R. to Waverly; Erie Railway to Niagara Falls; New York Central R. R. to Lewiston; steamer to Toronto, and Grand Trunk R. W. or Royal Mail Line Steamers to Montreal; *returning* via Grand Trunk R. W. to Rouse's Point; Lake Champlain Steamers to Ticonderoga; Stage to Lake George; Lake George Steamer to Caldwell; Stage to Glenn's Falls; Rens. & Saratoga R. R. to Saratoga and Albany; Hudson River Steamers to New York, and N. Y. Div. Penna. R. R. to Philadelphia..$39.20.

EXCURSION P 101.—*Philadelphia to Montreal and return to Philadelphia;* Same route as Excursion P 100, except that a visit from Plattsburg, on Lake Champlain, to Au Sable Chasm and return, is provided for..$41.45.

QUEBEC EXCURSIONS.

EXCURSION P 102.—*Philadelphia to Quebec and return to Philadelphia;* via North Penna. R. R. to Bethlehem; Lehigh Valley R. R. to Waverly; Erie Railway to Niagara Falls; New York Central R. R. to Lewiston; Steamer to Toronto, and Grand Trunk R. W. or Royal Mail Line Steamers to Quebec and back to Montreal; *returning* thence via Grand Trunk R. W. to Ronse's Point; Lake Champlain Steamer to Ticonderoga; Stage to Lake George; Lake George Steamer to Caldwell; Stage to Glenn's Falls; Rens. & Saratoga R. R. to Saratoga and Albany; Hudson River Steamers to New York, and N. Y. Div. Penna. R. R. to Philadelphia..$44.20.

EXCURSION P 103.—*Philadelphia to Quebec and return to Philadelphia;* via North Penna. R. R. to Bethlehem; Lehigh Valley R. R. to Waverly; Erie Railway to Niagara Falls; New York Central R. R. to Lewiston; Steamer to Toronto, and Grand Trunk R. W. or Royal Mail Line Steamers to Quebec; *returning* thence via Grand Trunk R. W. to Gorham; Stage to Glen House and Summit Mt. Washington; Mt. Washington R W. to Base; Stage to Crawford House and Fabyan House; Boston, Concord & Montreal R. R. to Bethlehem; Stage to Profile House and Littleton; Boston, Concord & Montreal R. R. to Wells River; Montpelier & Wells River R. R. to Montpelier; Central Vermont R. R. to Burlington; Lake Champlain Steamers to Ticonderoga; Stage to Lake George; Lake George Steamer to Caldwell; Stage to Glenn's Falls; Rens. & Saratoga R. R. to Saratoga and Albany; Hudson River Steamers to New York, and Penna. R. R. to Philadelphia.
$67.60.

OGDENSBURG EXCURSIONS.

EXCURSION P 114.—*Philadelphia to Ogdensburg and return to Philadelphia;* via North Penna. R. R. to Bethlehem; Lehigh Valley R. R. to Waverly; Erie Railway to Niagara Falls; New York Central R. R. to Lewiston; Steamer to Toronto, and Grand Trunk R. W. or Royal Mail Line Steamers to Ogdensburg; *returning* via Vt. Central R. R. to Rouse's Point; Lake Champlain Steamers to Whitehall; Rens. & Saratoga R. R. to Saratoga and Albany; Hudson River Steamers to New York, and N. Y. Div. Penna. R. R. to Philadelphia..$35.25.

EXCURSION P 115.—*Philadelphia to Ogdensburg and return to Philadelphia;* via North Penna. R. R. to Bethlehem; Lehigh Valley R. R. to Waverly; Erie Railway to Niagara Falls; New York Central R. R. to Lewiston; Steamer to Toronto, and Grand Trunk R. W. or Royal Mail Line Steamers to Ogdensburg; *returning* via Vt. Central R. R. to Rouse's Point; Lake Champlain Steamers to Ticonderoga; Stage to Lake George; Lake George Steamer to Caldwell; Stage to Glenn's Falls; Rens. & Saratoga R. R. to Saratoga and Albany; Hudson River Steamers to New York, and N. Y. Div. Penna. R. R. to Philadelphia..$38.20.

ALEXANDRIA BAY EXCURSIONS.

EXCURSION P 130.—*Philadelphia to Alexandria Bay and return to Philadelphia;* via North Penna. R. R. to Bethlehem; Lehigh Valley R. R. to Waverly; Erie Railway to Binghamton; D., L. & W. R. R. to Utica; Utica & Black River R. R. to Clayton, and Steamer to Alexandria Bay; *returning* via Steamer to Clayton; Utica & Black River R. R. to Utica; New York Central R. R. to Geneva; Seneca Lake Steamers to Watkins'; Nor. Cent. R. W. to Elmira; Erie Railway to Waverly; Lehigh Valley R. R. to Bethlehem, and North Penna. R. R. to Philadelphia...$24.80.

EXCURSION P 131.—*Philadelphia to Alexandria Bay and return to Philadelphia;* via North Penna. R. R. to Bethlehem; Lehigh Valley R. R. to Waverly; Erie Railway to Binghamton; D., L. & W. R. R. to Syracuse; Syracuse Northern R R. to Sandy Creek; Rome, Watertown & Ogdensburg R. R. to Cape Vincent, and Steamer to Alexandria Bay; *returning* via Steamer to Clayton; Utica & Black River R. R. to Utica; D., L. & W. R. R. to Binghamton, and thence to Manunka Chunk, and Penna. R. R. to Philadelphia.
$23.40.

WHITE MOUNTAINS EXCURSIONS.

EXCURSION P 104.—*Philadelphia to White Mountains and return to Philadelphia;* via North Penna. R. R. to Bethlehem; Lehigh Valley R. R. to Waverly; Erie Railway to Niagara Falls; New York Central R. R. to Lewiston; Steamer to Toronto, and Grand Trunk R. W. or Royal Mail Line Steamers to Montreal; thence via Grand Trunk R. W. to Rouse's Point; Lake Champlain Steamers to Burlington; Central Vermont R. R. to Montpelier; Montpelier & Wells River R. R. to Wells River; Boston, Concord & Montreal R. R. to Littleton; Stage to Profile House and Bethlehem; Boston, Concord & Montreal R. R. to Fabyan House; Stage to Crawford House and Base Mt. Washington; Mt. Washington R. W. to Summit; Stage to Glen House and Glen Station; Portland & Ogdensburg R. R. to Portland; Boston & Maine R. R. to Boston; Old Colony & Newport R. R. to Newport; Fall River Line Steamers to New York, and N. Y. Div. Penna. R. R. to Philadelphia..................$60.65.

EXCURSION P 105.—*Philadelphia to White Mountains and return to Philadelphia;* via North Penna. R. R. to Bethlehem; Lehigh Valley R. R. to Waverly; Erie Railway to Niagara Falls; New York Central R. R. to Lewiston; Steamer to Toronto, and Grand Trunk R. W. or Royal Mail Line Steamers to Montreal; thence via Grand Trunk R. W. to Lenoxville; Conn. & Pass. Rivers R. R. to Newport. Vt. and Wells River; Boston, Concord & Montreal R. R. to Littleton; Stage to Profile House and Bethlehem; Boston, Concord & Montreal R. R. to Fabyan House; Stage to Crawford House and Bemis'; Portland & Ogdensburg R. R. to Portland; Boston & Maine R. R. to Boston; Old Colony & Newport R. R to Newport; Fall River Line Steamers to New York, and Penna. R. R. to Philadelphia..................$50.75.

EXCURSION P 106.—*Philadelphia to White Mountains and return to Philadelphia;* via North Penna. R. R. to Bethlehem; Lehigh Valley R. R to Waverly; Erie Railway to Niagara Falls; New York Central R. R. to Lewiston; Steamer to Toronto, and Grand Trunk R. W. or Royal Mail Line Steamers to Quebec; thence via Grand Trunk R. W. to Lenoxville; Conn. & Pass. Rivers R. R. to Newport, Vt. and Wells River; Boston, Concord & Montreal R. R. to Littleton; Stage to Profile House and Bethlehem; Boston, Concord & Montreal R. R. to Fabyan House; Stage to Crawford House and back to Fabyan House; Boston, Concord & Montreal R. R. to Concord; Concord R. R. to Nashau; Boston, Lowell & Nashua R. R. to Boston; Old Colony & Newport R. R. to Newport; Fall River Line Steamers to New York, and Penna. R. R. to Philadelphia..................$55.15.

EXCURSION P 107.—*Philadelphia to White Mountains and return to Philadelphia;* via North Penna. R. R. to Bethlehem; Lehigh Valley R. R. to Waverly; Erie Railway to Niagara Falls; New York Central R. R. to Lewiston; Steamer to Tor nto, and Grand Trunk R. W. or Royal Mail Line Steamers to Quebec; thence via Grand Trunk R. W. to Gorham; Stage to Glen House, Summit Mt. Washington, and back to Glen House and Glen Station; Portland & Ogdensburg R. R. to Portland; Boston & Maine R. R. to Boston; Old Colony & Newport R. R. to Newport; Fall River Line Steamers to New York, and Penna. R. R. to Philadelphia..................$55.75.

EXCURSION P 108.—*Philadelphia to White Mountains and return to Philadelphia;* via North Penna. R. R. to Bethlehem; Lehigh Valley R. R. to Waverly; Erie Railway to Niagara Falls; New York Central R. R. to Lewiston; Steamer to Toronto, and Grand Trunk R. W. or Royal Mail Line Steamers to Montreal; thence via Grand Trunk R. W. to St. John's; South-eastern R. R. to Newport, Vt; Conn. & Pass. Rivers R. R. to Wells River; Boston, Concord & Montreal R. R. to Littleton; S age to Profile House and Bethlehem; Boston, Concord. and Montreal R. R. to Fabyan House; Stage to Crawford House and Bemis'; Portland & Ogdensburg R. R. to Portland; Boston & Maine R. R. to Boston; Old Colony & Newport R. R. to Newport; Fall River Line Steamers to New York, and Penna. R. R. to Philadelphia..................$50.75.

EXCURSION P 109.—*Philadelphia to White Mountains and return to Philadelphia;* via North Penna. R. R. to Bethlehem; Lehigh Valley R. R. to Waverly; Erie Railway to Niagara Falls; New York Central R. R. to Lewiston; Steamer to Toronto, and Grand Trunk R. W. or Royal Line Mail Steamers to Quebec; thence via Grand Trunk R. W. to Lenoxville; Conn. & Pass. Rivers R. R. to Newport, Vt. and Wells River; Boston, Concord & Montreal R. R. to Littleton; Stage to Profile House and Bethlehem; Boston, Concord, & Montreal R. R. to Fabyan House; Stage to Crawford House and back to Fabyan House; Boston, Concord, & Montreal R. R. to Concord. & Pass. Rivers R. R. to Springfield; Central Vermont R. R. to South Vernon; Conn. River R. R. to Springfield; N. Y., N. H. & H. R. R. to New York, and Penna. R. R. to Philadelphia..................$53.90.

EXCURSION P 110.—*Philadelphia to White Mountains and return to Philadelphia;* via North Penna. R. R. to Bethlehem; Lehigh Valley R. R. to Waverly; Erie Railway to Niagara Falls; New York Central R. R. to Lewiston; Steamer to Toronto, and Grand Trunk R. W. or Royal Mail Line Steamers to Montreal; thence via Grand Trunk R. W. to Lenoxville; Conn. & Pass. Rivers R. R. to Newport, Vt. and Wells River; Boston, Concord & Montreal R. R. to Littleton; Stage to Profile House and Bethlehem; Boston, Concord & Montreal R. R. to Fabyan House; Stage to Base Mt. Washington; Mt. Washington R. W. to Summit and back to Base Mt. Washington; Stage to Crawford House and Bemis'; Portland & Ogdensburg R. R. to North Conway; Eastern R. R. to Wolfboro; Steamer to Weirs; Boston, Concord & Montreal R. R. to Concord; Concord R. R. to Nashua; Boston, Lowell & Nashua R. R. to Boston; Old Colony and Newport R. R. to Newport; Fall River Line Steamers to New York, and Penna. R. R. to Philadelphia..............$59.50.

EXCURSION P 111.—*Philadelphia to White Mountains and return to Philadelphia;* via North Penna. R. R. to Bethlehem; Lehigh Valley R. R. to Waverly; Erie Railway to Niagara Falls; New York Central R. R. to Lewiston; Steamer to Toronto, and Grand Trunk R. W. or Royal Mail Line Steamers to Montreal; thence via Grand Trunk R. W. to Lenoxville; Conn. & Pass. Rivers R. R. to Newport, Vt. and Wells River; Boston, Concord & Montreal R. R. to Littleton; Stage to Profile House and Bethlehem; Boston, Concord & Montreal R. R. to Fabyan House; Stage to Crawford House and Bemis'; Portland and Ogdensburg R. R. to North Conway; Eastern R. R. to Boston; Old Colony & Newport R. R. to Newport; Fall River Line Steamers to New York, and Penna. R. R. to Philadelphia.................$50.75.

EXCURSION P 112.—*Philadelphia to White Mountains and return to Philadelphia;* via North Penna. R. R. to Bethlehem; Lehigh Valley R. R. to Waverly; Erie Railway to Niagara Falls; New York Central R. R. to Lewiston; Steamer to Toronto and Grand Trunk R. W. or Royal Mail Line Steamers to Quebec; thence via Grand Trunk R. W. to Gorham; Stage to Glen House and North Conway; Eastern R. R. to Boston; Old Colony & Newport R. R. to Newport, Fall River Line Steamers to New York, and Penna. R. R. to Philadelphia................$48.25.

EXCURSION P 113.—*Philadelphia to White Mountains and return to Philadelphia;* via North Penna. R. R. to Bethlehem; Lehigh Valley R. R. to Waverly; Erie Railway to Niagara Falls; New York Central R. R. to Lewiston; Steamer to Toronto. and Grand Trunk R. W. or Royal Mail Line Steamers to Montreal; thence via Grand Trunk R. W. to St. John's; South-eastern R. R. to Newport, Vt.; Conn. & Pass. Rivers R. R. to Wells River; Boston, Concord & Montreal R. R. to Littleton; Stage to Profile House and Bethlehem; Boston, Concord & Montreal R. R. to Fabyan House; Stage to Crawford House and Base Mt. Washington; Mt. Washington R. W. to Summit; Stage to Glen House and North Conway; Eastern R. R. to Boston; Old Colony & Newport R. R. to Newport, Fall River Line Steamers to New York, and Penna. R. R. to Philadelphia..............$60.25.

EXCURSION P 125.—*Philadelphia to White Mountains and return to Philadelphia;* via North Penna. R. R. to Bethlehem; Lehigh Valley R. R. to Waverly; Erie Railway to Niagara Falls; New York Central R. R. to Schenectady; Rens. & Saratoga R. R. to Glenn's Falls; Stage to Caldwell; Lake George Steamer to Ticonderoga; Stage to Ti Landing; Lake Champlain Steamers to Burlington; Central Vermont R. R. to Montpelier; Montpelier & Wells River R. R. to Wells River; Boston, Concord & Montreal R. R. to Fabyan House; Stage to Base Mt. Washington; Mt. Washington R. W. to Summit and back to Base; Stage to Crawford House and Fabyan House; Boston, Concord & Montreal R. R. to Bethlehem; Stage to Profile House; Stage or Rail to Plymouth; Boston, Concord & Montreal R. R. to Concord; Concord R. R. to Nashua; Boston. Lowell & Nashua R. R. to Boston; Old Colony and Newport R. R. to Newport, Fall River Line Steamers to New York, and Penna. R. R. to Philadelphia...............$55.65.

EXCURSION P 126.—*Philadelphia to White Mountains and return to Philadelphia;* via North Penna. R. R. to Bethlehem; Lehigh Valley R. R. to Waverly; Erie Railway to Niagara Falls; New York Central R. R. to Lewiston; Steamer to Toronto, and Grand Trunk R. W. or Royal Mail Line Steamers to Montreal; thence via Grand Trunk R. W. to Rouse's Point; Lake Champlain Steamers to Burlington; Central Vermont R. R. to Montpelier; Montpelier & Wells River R. R. to Wells River; Boston, Concord & Montreal R. R. to Fabyan House; Stage to Base Mt. Washington; Mt. Washington R. W. to Summit and back to Base; Stage to Crawford House and Bemis'; Portland & Ogdensburg R. R. to North Conway; Eastern R. R. to Boston; Old Colony & Newport R. R. to' Newport; Fall River Line Steamers to New York, and Penna. R. R. to Philadelphia..............$55.65.

EXCURSION P 127.—*Philadelphia to White Mountains and return to Philadelphia;* via North Penna. R. R. to Bethlehem; Lehigh Valley R. R. to Waverly; Erie Railway to Niagara Falls; New York Central R. R. to Lewiston; Steamer to Toronto, and Grand Trunk R. W. or Royal Mail Line Steamers to Montreal; thence via Grand Trunk R. W. to Gorham; Stage to Glen House and Summit of Mt. Washington; Mt. Washington R. W. to Base; Stage to Fabyan House; Boston, Concord & Montreal R. R. to Bethlehem; Stage to Profile House; Stage or Rail to Plymouth; Boston, Concord & Montreal R. R. to Concord; Concord R. R. to Nashua; Boston, Lowell & Nashua R. R. to Boston; Old Colony & Newport R. R. to Newport; Fall River Line Steamers to New York, and Penna. R. R. to Philadelphia..$61.40.

EXCURSION P 128.—*Philadelphia to White Mountains and return to Philadelphia;* via North Penna. R. R. to Bethlehem; Lehigh Valley R. R. to Waverly; Erie Railway to Niagara Falls; New York Central R. R. to Lewiston; Steamer to Toronto, and Grand Trunk R. W. or Royal Mail Line Steamers to Montreal; thence via Grand Trunk R. W. to Groveton Junction; Boston, Concord & Montreal R. R. to Fabyan House; Stage to base Mt. Washington; Mt. Washington R. W. to summit; Stage to Glen House and North Conway: Eastern R. R. to Boston; Fall River Line Steamers to New York, and Penna. R. R. to Philadelphia..$53.20.

JNO. N. ABBOTT,
Gen'l Passenger Agent Erie Railway,
NEW YORK.

N. VAN HORN,
South-eastern Passenger Agent Erie Railway,
732 CHESTNUT STREET, PHILADELPHIA.

EXCURSION ROUTES

AND

RATES OF FARE

VIA

LEHIGH VALLEY AND NORTH PENNSYLVANIA RAILROADS.

EXCURSION TICKETS ARE GOOD DURING THE PLEASURE SEASON, (JUNE 1ST TO NOVEMBER 1ST,) UNLESS OTHERWISE LIMITED, AND HAVE ALL THE PRIVILEGES OF FIRST CLASS TICKETS.

Philadelphia to Easton and return; via North Penna. and Lehigh Valley Railroads in both directions..$3.00.

Philadelphia to Freemansburg and return; via North Penna. and Lehigh Valley Railroads in both directions..$2.65.

Philadelphia to Allentown and return; via North Penna. and Lehigh Valley Railroads in both directions..$2.75.

Philadelphia to Catasauqua and return; via North Penna. and Lehigh Valley Railroads in both directions..$2.90.

Philadelphia to Hokendauqua and return; via North Penna. and Lehigh Valley Railroads in both directions..$2.95.

Philadelphia to Coplay and return; via North Penna. and Lehigh Valley Railroads in both directions..$3.00.

Philadelphia to White Hall and return; via North Penna. and Lehigh Valley Railroads in both directions..$3.05.

Philadelphia to Laury's and return; via North Penna. and Lehigh Valley Railroads in both directions..$3.20.

Philadelphia to Rockdale and return; via North Penna. and Lehigh Valley Railroads in both directions..$3.35.

Philadelphia to Slatington and return; via North Penna. and Lehigh Valley Railroads in both directions..$3.55.

Philadelphia to Lehigh Gap and return; via North Penna. and Lehigh Valley Railroads in both directions..$3.70.

Philadelphia to Parryville and return; via North Penna. and Lehigh Valley Railroads in both directions..$3.90

Philadelphia to Lehighton and return; via North Penna. and Lehigh Valley Railroads in both directions..$4.00.

Philadelphia to Mauch Chunk and return; via North Penna. and Lehigh Valley Railroads in both directions..$4.20.

Philadelphia to Switchback and return; via North Penna. and Lehigh Valley Railroads, Omnibus, and Mauch Chunk & Summit Hill Railroad in both directions..........$5.00.

Philadelphia to Switchback and Glen Onoko and return; via North Penna. and Lehigh Valley Railroads, Omnibus, and Mauch Chunk & Summit Hill Railroad in both directions..$5.25.

Philadelphia to Penn Haven Junction and return; via North Penna. and Lehigh Valley Railroads in both directions..........$4.55.

Philadelphia to Weatherly and return; via North Penna. and Lehigh Valley Railroads in both directions..........$5.10.

Philadelphia to Beaver Meadow and return; via North Penna. and Lehigh Valley Railroads in both directions..........$5.40.

Philadelphia to Jeansville and return; via North Penna. and Lehigh Valley Railroads in both directions..........$5.55.

Philadelphia to Audenried and return; via North Penna. and Lehigh Valley Railroads in both directions..........$5.60.

Philadelphia to Eckley and return; via North Penna. and Lehigh Valley Railroads in both directions..........$5.50.

Philadelphia to Jeddo and return; via North Penna. and Lehigh Valley Railroads in both directions..........$5.55.

Philadelphia to Hazleton and return; via North Penna. and Lehigh Valley Railroads in both directions..........$5.40.

Philadelphia to Catawissa and return; via North Penna., Lehigh Valley, and Penna. Railroads in both directions..........$5.80.

Philadelphia to Danville and return; via North Penna., Lehigh Valley, and Penna. Railroads in both directions..........$6.20.

Philadelphia to Sunbury and return; via North Penna., Lehigh Valley, and Penna. Railroads in both directions..........$6.70.

Philadelphia to Williamsport and return; via North Penna., Lehigh Valley, and Penna. Railroads in both directions..........$8.00.

Philadelphia to Mahanoy City and return; via North Penna. and Lehigh Valley Railroads in both directions..........$4.35.

Philadelphia to Shenandoah and return; via North Penna. and Lehigh Valley Railroads in both directions..........$4.85.

Philadelphia to Centralia and return; via North Penna. and Lehigh Valley Railroads in both directions..........$5.00.

Philadelphia to Mount Carmel and return; via North Penna. and Lehigh Valley Railroads in both directions..........$5.15.

Philadelphia to White Haven and return; via North Penna. and Lehigh Valley Railroads in both directions..........$5.40.

Philadelphia to Wilkesbarre and return; via North Penna. and Lehigh Valley Railroads in both directions..........$6.90.

Philadelphia to Pittston and return; via North Penna. and Lehigh Valley Railroads in both directions..........$7.00.

Philadelphia to Lackawanna Junction and return; via North Penna. and Lehigh Valley Railroads in both directions..........$7.00.

Philadelphia to Elmira and return; via North Penna. and Lehigh Valley Railroads in both directions..........$10.70.

Philadelphia to Ithaca and return; via North Penna., Lehigh Valley, and Ithaca & Athens Railroads in both directions..........$11.35.

Philadelphia to Auburn and return; via North Penna., Lehigh Valley, and Southern Central Railroads in both directions..........$12.00.

SIDE-TRIP OR EXTENSION EXCURSIONS

ISSUED BY THE

ERIE RAILWAY COMPANY.

EXCURSION A.—*Elmira to Watkins' Glen and return to Elmira;* via Northern Central R. R. in both directions..$1.30.

EXCURSION B.—*Albany to Whitehall and return to Albany;* via Rens. & Saratoga R. R. to Saratoga and Glenn's Falls; Stage to Lake George; Lake George Steamer to Ticonderoga; Stage to Lake Champlain, and Lake Champlain Steamers to Whitehall; *returning* via Rens. & Saratoga R. R. via Saratoga to Albany...$9.40.

EXCURSION C.—*Albany to Whitehall and return to Albany;* via Rens. & Saratoga R. R. to Saratoga and Whitehall; *returning* via Lake Champlain Steamers to Ti. Landing; Stage to Ticonderoga; Lake George Steamer to Caldwell; Stage to Glenn's Falls, and Rens. and Saratoga R. R. via Saratoga to Albany...$9.40.

EXCURSION D.—*New York to Philadelphia (with privilege of stopping over at Long Branch);* via N. J. Southern R. R. Steamers to Sandy Hook; New Jersey Southern R. R. to Pemberton Junc., and Penna. R. R. to Philadelphia...$2.25.

EXCURSION E.—*Mauch Chunk to Summit Hill and return to Mauch Chunk;* via Switchback R. R., including omnibus transfer between hotel and depot.................................$1.40.

EXCURSION F.—*Plattsburg (Fouquet's Hotel) to Au Sable Chasm and return to Plattsburg*.....$2.25.

EXCURSION G.—*Montreal to Quebec and return to Montreal;* via Grand Trunk Railway or Royal Mail Line Steamers in both directions..$5.00.

EXCURSION H.—*Quebec to Ha-Ha Bay and return to Quebec;* via Grand Trunk Railway; Steamers in both directions...$9.00.

EXCURSION I.—*Elmira to Geneva (on Seneca Lake) and return to Elmira;* via Northern Central R. R. to Watkins', and Seneca Lake Steamers to Geneva; *returning* by same route...$2.80.

N. VAN HORN,
South eastern Passenger Agent, Phila.

JNO. N. ABBOTT,
General Passenger Agent, New York.

SEWING-MACHINE SALES OF 1873.

The table of Sewing-machine sales for 1873 shows that our sales last year amounted to **232,444** (two hundred and thirty-two thousand four hundred and forty-four) machines, being a large increase over the sales of the previous year (1872).

The table also shows that our sales **Exceed those of any other Company,** for the period named, by the number of **113,254 machines,** or nearly double those of any other Company.

It may be further stated that the sales of 1873, as compared with those of 1872, show a relatively larger increase, beyond the sales of other makers, than of any other year.

For instance, in 1872 we sold 45,000 more Machines than any other company, whereas, in 1873, the sales were

113,254 Machines in Excess of our Highest Competitor.

These figures are all the more remarkable for the reason that the sales of the principal companies in 1873 are **less than their sales in 1872**; whereas, as has been shown, **our sales have largely increased.**

The account of sales is from sworn returns made to the owners of the Sewing-Machine Patents.

It will hardly be denied that the superiority of the **SINGER MACHINES** is fully demonstrated—at all events, that their popularity in the household is unquestionable.

THE SINGER MANUFACTURING COMPANY,
34 UNION SQUARE, NEW YORK.

Philadelphia Office, No. 1106 Chestnut Street.

SALES OF 1873.

Company	Machines
The Singer Manufacturing Company,	Sold 232,444
Wheeler & Wilson Manufacturing Company,	" 119,190
Domestic Sewing-Machine Company,	" 40,114
Grover & Baker Sewing-Machine Company,	" 36,179
Weed Sewing-Machine Company,	" 21,769
Wilson Sewing-Machine Company,	" 21,247
Howe Machine Company,	" no returns.
Gold Medal Sewing-Machine Company,	" 16,431
Wilcox & Gibbs Sewing-Machine Company,	" 15,881
American Button-hole, &c.,	" 14,182
B. P. Howe Sewing-Machine Company,	" 13,919
Remington Empire Sewing-Machine Company,	" 9,183
Florence Sewing-Machine Company,	" 8,960
Davies Sewing-Machine Company,	" 8,861
Victor Sewing-Machine Company,	" 7,446
Blees Sewing-Machine Company,	" 3,458
Secor Sewing-Machine Company,	" 4,430
Ætna, J. F. Braunsdorf & Co.,	" 3,081
Bartram & Fanton,	" 1,000
Centennial Sewing-Machine Company,	" 514
Keystone Sewing-Machine Company,	" 217

☞ Secure Drawing-room Car Accommodations superior to those of any other Line.

PALACE CARS
FROM PHILADELPHIA
TO

NIAGARA FALLS
VIA THE
NORTH PENNSYLVANIA,
LEHIGH VALLEY,
AND ERIE RAILWAYS.

THE ELEGANT PARLOR CARS

OF THE
PENNSYLVANIA & NEW YORK DRAWING-ROOM CAR COMPANY

ARE ATTACHED TO THE

8.30 A. M. Fast Line from Philadelphia

FOR

| BUFFALO, | ELMIRA, | ALLENTOWN, |
| NIAGARA FALLS, | WILKESBARRE, | BETHLEHEM, |

And Intermediate Stations, arriving at Niagara Falls the same evening.

☞ These Cars are fitted up in the most elaborate manner, being furnished with Separate Compartments, Revolving Cushioned Arm-chairs, and all the comforts and conveniences calculated to make traveling a pleasure.

SEATS MAY BE SECURED IN ADVANCE AT THE

Offices, 732 Chestnut Street, 105 South Fifth Street,

PHILADELPHIA,

And at the North Pennsylvania Passenger Depot, Berks and American Streets, on the morning of departure.

ELLIS CLARK,
General Agent Penna. & New York Drawing-Room Car Company.

1874.   TO   1874.
TOURISTS AND PLEASURE-SEEKERS.

IMPROVED ARRANGEMENT.

CANADIAN NAVIGATION COMPANY'S
LINES OF THROUGH STEAMERS.

NIAGARA FALLS TO MONTREAL, QUEBEC, WHITE MOUNTAINS, PORTLAND, LAKE GEORGE, SARATOGA, NEW YORK, RIVIERE DU LOUP, THE RIVER SAGUENAY, &c.

The Canadian Navigation Company's Steamers comprise the original Royal Mail and American Lines, with the addition of several new Steamers, thus forming two first-class lines of Passenger Steamers which, for speed, safety, and comfort, cannot be surpassed.

They are the only lines now affording Tourists an opportunity to view the magnificent scenery of the Thousand Islands and Rapids of St. Lawrence, also to the far-famed River Saguenay.

☞ This Route possesses peculiar advantages over any other, as by it parties *have their choice of either side of Lake Ontario and River St. Lawrence, between Niagara Falls and Quebec*, over the whole or any portion of it, without being obliged to decide when purchasing their tickets, as they are also good by the Grand Trunk Railway. No extra charge for Meals on the Steamers between Toronto and Montreal.

The only route to the White Mountains by which parties can ascend the far-famed Mount Washington by the carriage road.

American money taken at par for tickets by this line, which can be obtained at most of the principal cities in the United States.

E. BARBER,   ALEX. MILLOY,
AGENT,   SECRETARY CANADIAN NAVIGATION COMPANY,
Niagara Falls, N. Y.   *Office, St. James Street, Montreal.*

1874. LAKE CHAMPLAIN AND LAKE GEORGE. 1874.

THE FASHIONABLE THOROUGHFARE AND
PLEASURE ROUTE
BETWEEN
MONTREAL AND NEW YORK
VIA
LAKE CHAMPLAIN, LAKE GEORGE, AND SARATOGA.

TWO EXPRESS TRAINS DAILY

From Montreal, connecting at ROUSE'S POINT with the elegant and commodious Lake Champlain Steamers

"VERMONT,"  "CHAMPLAIN,"
Capt. Wm. H. Flagg. Capt. Geo. Rushlow.

"ADIRONDACK," "A. WILLIAMS,"
Capt. Wm. Anderson. Capt. B. J. Holt.

FORMING TWO DAILY LINES

Each way through the lake, connecting at Ticonderoga with steamer "MINNEHAHA," through Lake George, and at Whitehall with trains of Reusselaer & Saratoga Railroad for Saratoga, Troy, Albany, and New York.

ONLY ROUTE to LAKE GEORGE and ONLY DIRECT ROUTE to SARATOGA.

Tickets and information furnished at the principal agencies of the Erie, New York Central, Hudson River, and Grand Trunk Railroads, in New York, Philadelphia, Baltimore, St. Louis, Chicago, Niagara Falls, Montreal, and at the principal stations of all connecting lines.

☞ Be sure that your ticket reads via ROUSE'S POINT and LAKE CHAMPLAIN, as the connection is always sure.

J. N. BOCKUS,   A. L. INMAN,
Agent,   *General Superintendent.*
St. Lawrence Hall Building, Montreal.

MICHIGAN CENTRAL & GREAT WESTERN
RAILWAYS,
VIA NIAGARA FALLS,

In direct connection, at SUSPENSION BRIDGE and BUFFALO, with all Express Trains on the NEW YORK CENTRAL & HUDSON RIVER and ERIE RAILWAYS, for

ST. CATHARINE'S, HAMILTON, TORONTO, LONDON, SARNIA, DETROIT, GRAND RAPIDS, MUSKEGON, PENTWATER, CHICAGO, MILWAUKEE, ST. PAUL, ST. LOUIS, SAN FRANCISCO,

And all points in the WEST, NORTH-WEST, and SOUTH-WEST.

EQUIPMENT FIRST-CLASS! WESTINGHOUSE AIR BRAKES! MILLER'S COUPLING AND PLATFORM!

At Hamilton and Toronto connections are made daily, (Sundays excepted,) during the Summer Season, with the

Splendid Royal Mail Line of Steamers
FOR
MONTREAL, QUEBEC,

And principal points on Lake Ontario and the River St. Lawrence.

THE ONLY ROUTE TO THE WEST
VIA NIAGARA FALLS AND DETROIT,

Running the Pullman and Wagner Palace Sleeping and Drawing-room Cars to Chicago without change, and the only route which enables passengers to view from the cars

"THE FALLS AND SCENERY OF NIAGARA"
While crossing the Mammoth Suspension Bridge.

☞ The celebrated Pullman Hotel and Dining Car leaves Rochester *daily* for Chicago, without change.

Ask for Tickets via Niagara Falls and the Great Western and Michigan Central Railways, which are good until used, and allow passengers to stop off and resume their journey at pleasure.

A. J. HARLOW,   WM. EDGAR,
General Eastern Passenger Agent,   General Ticket Accountant.
349 Broadway, (cor. Leonard Street,) New York.

THE TRAVELING PUBLIC PRONOUNCE
THE
CHICAGO, BURLINGTON & QUINCY
RAILROAD
THE FAVORITE ROUTE
FROM
CHICAGO to the WEST

PULLMAN'S HOTEL CARS ON ALL EXPRESS TRAINS.

YOU WILL FIND TICKETS VIA THIS FAVORITE ROUTE AT ALL OFFICES IN THE WEST.

SAN FRANCISCO EXPRESS.

PULLMAN'S SIXTEEN-WHEELED SLEEPING CARS ARE RUN ON THE

If you propose to visit MISSOURI, IOWA, NEBRASKA, KANSAS, COLORADO, UTAH, or CALIFORNIA, BUY YOUR TICKETS VIA C., B. & Q. R. R. They can be had at all through Ticket Offices in the East, and at the OFFICE of the COMPANY, 317 BROADWAY, NEW YORK, and at the Depot, foot of Lake Street, Chicago. For Maps or information, address

J. Q. A. BEAN,   or   D. W. HITCHCOCK,
GENERAL FREIGHT AGENT,   GENERAL PASSENGER AGENT,
Chicago, Ill.   102 Michigan Avenue, Chicago.

DELAWARE & HUDSON CANAL COMPANY,

Lessee of the

ALBANY & SUSQUEHANNA
RENSSELAER & SARATOGA } **RAILROADS,**

AND

LAKE GEORGE
AND
LAKE CHAMPLAIN } **STEAMERS.**

THE ONLY ROUTE

VIA

BINGHAMTON, ALBANY, TROY, SCHENECTADY, RUTLAND, or ROUSE'S POINT,

TO

COOPERSTOWN, SHARON SPRINGS,

HOWE'S CAVE, BALLSTON SPA,

SARATOGA SPRINGS,

THE ADIRONDACK AND WHITE MOUNTAINS,

AND ALL POINTS ON

LAKE GEORGE and LAKE CHAMPLAIN;

ALSO,

42 Miles the Shortest Route between New York and Montreal.

For rates, tickets, or information, apply to Ticket Agents of any connecting line, or to the undersigned.

S. E. MAYO,
Gen'l Passenger Agent,
Albany, N. Y.

FOUQUET'S HOTEL

PLATTSBURGH, N. Y.

This Hotel has always been the favorite resting-place for travelers between Niagara Falls, Lake George, and Saratoga. It is situated

ON THE BANKS OF LAKE CHAMPLAIN,
AMID A BEAUTIFUL GARDEN OF FLOWERS.

Parties going southward, who desire to SEE LAKE CHAMPLAIN BY DAYLIGHT, should be particular to leave Montreal by the P. M. train which connects with Lake Champlain steamer, arriving at "Fouquet's" for supper. Leaving Plattsburgh by steamer the following morning, they will arrive at Caldwell for supper, or, if they prefer, can continue through the lake to Whitehall, and arrive at Saratoga for supper. This House is also the principal starting point for the Adirondacks, and is situated only twelve miles from the WONDERFUL AU SABLE CHASM, one of those great natural curiosities which, to the lover of nature in all her fanciful moods, presents such attractions. It is through this gorge that the waters of the Au Sable seek and finally mingle with those of Lake Champlain. The changing beauty of this stream, as it bounds from ledge to ledge, passing through this wonderful freak of nature, adds to the surrounding scenery a charm that all should see, and none will fail to appreciate.

Excursion Tickets are now on sale at the principal Railroad offices throughout the United States. Tickets are also on sale for Paul Smith's, Martin's, and other forest resorts in the Adirondacks, at the same offices.

STONINGTON LINE

BETWEEN
NEW YORK AND BOSTON.

THE ONLY INSIDE ROUTE, *via Providence,*
AVOIDING THE DANGERS OF POINT JUDITH.

The New and Elegant Steamers

RHODE ISLAND,
Capt. WM. M. JONES,

Narragansett,
Capt. RAY ALLEN.

Stonington,
Capt. JESSE MOTT,

Form the Finest Fleet of Sound Steamers leaving New York.

Not a trip missed in 6 years!

Daily, from Pier 33, N. R., foot Jay St., AT 5 P. M.

THROUGH TICKETS to all EASTERN POINTS, via this reliable route, can be obtained at all principal Ticket Offices throughout the country.

SPECIAL NOTICE. The New and Magnificent Steamer **Rhode Island** will, on and after JUNE **22d** next, leave Pier **30**, North River, foot Chambers Street, at **12** o'clock, Noon, and Pier foot **23d** Street, East River, **1** P. M., arriving in Boston the same evening, affording Passengers a sail through

LONG ISLAND SOUND BY DAYLIGHT.

TICKETS FOR SALE AT 732 CHESTNUT ST., PHILAD'A.

L. W. FILKINS,   D. S. BABCOCK,
General Passenger Agent.   *President.*

RATHBUN HOUSE,

ELMIRA, N. Y.   **E. R. ABBOTT, Proprietor.**   **M. J. BENSON, W. T. CHADBURN,** Clerks.

Mr. ABBOTT assumed control of the RATHBUN HOUSE, in the city of Elmira, one of the *best known and most popular Hotels* on the line of the Erie Railway, on the 4th of February, 1874, and it will continue to be kept as a **First-class Hotel in all respects.**

The Proprietor is a well-known Hotel man, his name being a sufficient guarantee that guests will be cared for with a regard chiefly directed to their comfort.

Business men traveling will be taken care of at prices to which they are accustomed through the country. The Rathbun House is in the centre of the business portion of the city, and these gentlemen will find it the most convenient house for them in Elmira.

A **Free 'Bus** will run to and from the Hotel and Depot to all trains.
☞ Baggage also free.

BENJAMIN C. HOPPER,

DEALER IN

DIAMONDS, WATCHES, CLOCKS, JEWELRY,

SILVER AND PLATED WARE,

No. 1320 CHESTNUT STREET,

PHILADELPHIA.

Particular attention given to repairing all kinds of Watches, Clocks, Music Boxes, and Jewelry.

Sole Agent for ORLEINE for cleaning Gold, Silver, and Plated Ware.

SENECA LAKE
STEAM NAVIGATION CO.

W. T. HAMILTON, President. JOHN LANG, Treasurer.
S. T. ARNOT, Vice-President. D. P. DEY, Superintendent.

STEAMERS
ONONDAGA, D. S. MAGEE, ELMIRA,
SCHUYLER, AND ONTARIO,

Are arranged to run during the season of pleasure travel, over Seneca Lake, making

SIX PASSAGES DAILY,
BETWEEN
WATKINS' and GENEVA

Leaving WATKINS' at 6.00 A. M., and 1.50 and 6.00 P. M.,

Connecting at Geneva with New York Central & Hudson River R. R., for Niagara Falls, the River St. Lawrence, Saratoga, Sharon Springs, and all places of summer resort.

To the tourist, Seneca Lake presents unusual attractions, being the most beautiful sheet of water on the continent, and navigable the whole year round. Its length is about forty miles, and in the passage over it scenes of stirring interest and romantic beauty are constantly presented.

WATKINS' GLEN,

Famed for its varied, wild, and picturesque scenery, is situated at the head of Seneca Lake, while Geneva, at its foot, is a place of considerable distinction as a Summer retreat.

Tickets over Seneca Lake, via Watkins' and Geneva, to Niagara Falls and all places of interest to Summer Excursionists, may be obtained at the offices of the ERIE RAILWAY, in New York, Philadelphia, and Boston.

A NEW CONVENIENCE for TRAVELERS.

The want of a Night Express Train, leaving Philadelphia by way of the North Pennsylvania and Lehigh Valley Railways at an early hour in the evening, and connecting at Elmira with the Fast Pacific Express for the West, on the Erie Railway, has long been felt, and is now to be supplied.

On and after SUNDAY EVENING, JUNE 14th, 1874,

AN EXPRESS TRAIN,
WITH
PULLMAN SLEEPING CARS ATTACHED,

Will leave the BERKS STREET DEPOT at 7 P. M. daily,

RUNNING THROUGH WITHOUT CHANGE,

Reaching Wilkesbarre about midnight and Elmira at 6.00 A. M., there connecting with the Erie Pacific Express, arriving at Niagara Falls at early dinner time, or about 1.00 o'clock. By this train, also, passengers may take the morning train north from Elmira and breakfast at Watkins' Glen; while those who live at points nearer this end of the line will find the evening train a rapid and convenient means of returning to their homes after transacting their business during the day in the city. By this route, it will be observed, also, there is but one change of coaches necessary between

PHILADELPHIA
AND
NIAGARA FALLS,   **CHICAGO,**
DETROIT,   **CINCINNATI,**
CLEVELAND,   **Or ST. LOUIS.**

It can thus easily be seen that the train will prove a popular one, and result in a travel which will amply reward the enterprise of the Managers.

TICKETS AND ALL INFORMATION MAY BE HAD AT THE COMPANY'S OFFICE,

No. 732 Chestnut Street, Philadelphia.

HALE, KILBURN & CO.'S
DUST SHIELD AND VENTILATOR
FOR STEAM CAR WINDOWS.

Sure Protection against Dust, Smoke, and Cinders.

RESPONSIBLE

AGENTS

WANTED

In every City

OF THE

UNITED STATES.

WILL BE SENT

BY MAIL

To any Address,

POSTPAID,

On Receipt of Price,

75 CENTS.

(Patented December 30th, 1873.)

UNFORTUNATE SUFFERER.—"Oh, dear! this car dust and those hot cinders! I am almost blind! and just look at my clothes,—nothing but dirt from head to foot."

LADY AND GENTLEMAN.—"Why, my dear sir, what is the matter? You appear very restless and unhappy. We think this delightful riding. We only paid the news-boy **75 Cents for this DUST SHIELD and VENTILATOR**, just as you see it here in the window, and oh, what a comfort! No more inflamed eyes, no more colds, and no more trouble from dust, smoke, cinders, or rain. Take our advice and procure one of the **New Shields** at once, and we'll warrant your misery to cease and your journey to become a pleasure."

WE WARRANT IT

To keep out of the window to which it is attached all DUST, SMOKE, and CINDERS, and to create a counter-current of air.

This is the most useful device ever invented for the traveling public, and it can be truly called the Tourist's Friend.

PRICE, 75 CENTS.

Sent by Mail to any address, postage prepaid, on receipt of price.

This Dust Shield being made of Fancy Wooden Slats, presents a neat and attractive appearance. It rolls up to the small space of about one inch in diameter, thus making it very convenient to carry in a satchel, shawl-strap, or a suitable pocket.

All orders addressed to us or to our Agents will receive prompt attention.

(OPEN.)   (CLOSED.)

P. O. Box 2138.   **HALE, KILBURN & CO.,**
Sole Proprietors and Manufacturers for the U. S.,
48 and 50 North Sixth St., and 615, 617, 619, and 621 Filbert St., Philad'a, Pa.

www.ingramcontent.com/pod-product-compliance
Lightning Source LLC
Chambersburg PA
CBHW022143090426
42742CB00010B/1374